ADULT EDUCATION AND ADULT LEARNING

Knud Illeris

ADULT EDUCATION AND ADULT LEARNING

KRIEGER PUBLISHING COMPANY

Knud Illeris
Adult Education and Adult Learning

Revised and translated into English by: Knud Illeris and Margaret Malone
from the Danish Edition:
Voksenuddannelse og Voksenlæring,
Roskilde University Press / Roskilde Universitetsforlag, 2003

First English Edition 2004

Printed and Published by
KRIEGER PUBLISHING COMPANY
KRIEGER DRIVE
MALABAR, FLORIDA 32950

FROM A DECLARATION OF PRINCIPLES JOINTLY ADOPTED BY A COMMITTEE OF THE AMERICAN BAR ASSOCIATION AND A COMMITTEE OF PUBLISHERS:
This publication is designed to provide accurate and authoritative information in regard to the subject matter covered. It is sold with the understanding that the publisher is not engaged in rendering legal, accounting, or other professional service. If legal advice or other expert assistance is required, the services of a competent professional person should be sought.

Library of Congress Cataloging-in-Publication Data

Illeris, Knud.
    [Voksenuddannelse og voksenlæring. English]
    Adult education and adult learning / Knud Illeris ; [revised and translated into English by Knud Illeris and Margaret Malone].—1st English
        p. cm.
    Translated from Danish.
    Includes bibliographical references (p.) and index.
    ISBN 1-57524-257-5 (alk. paper)
    1. Adult education—Denmark. 2. Adult learning—Denmark. I. Title.

    LC5256.D4I44   2004
    374—dc22

                                                                2004048436

    10 9 8 7 6 5 4 3 2

Contents

Part 2: Adult learning

Part 3: The practice of adult education programmes

Part 4: Adult education programmes today

PREFACE

This book is an attempt to summarise the general picture of adult education and adult learning that I have gradually developed in the course of over 30 years' engagement in research, development work, teaching, teacher training and debate about adult education and learning.

It has taken a rather long time to write the book and the story is a little unusual. The end of 2000 saw the completion of the "Adult Education Project", financed by the Danish Ministry of Education and the National Labour Market Authority and with me as head of research. The project had to do with the way in which participants in the broad Danish adult education programmes – adult vocational training, adult education centres and the day high schools – experience their educational situation and how they relate to it. The conclusions created quite a stir, documenting as they did some rather ambivalent attitudes on the part of the participants that are a far cry from the notions about well-motivated learners who are thirsting for knowledge and enlightenment – notions that have been dominant in connection with the modern slogan about lifelong learning.

This was why I wanted to write a more general book that would combine experience from this project and from the earlier General Qualification project in the field of adult vocational training (1992-97) with my theoretical insights into learning processes as put forward in my book entitled "The Three Dimensions of Learning", which was published in Danish in 1999 and in English translation in 2002. I set out on this work during spring 2001 and managed to write the first draft of what now comprises the first part of the present book. But I was also engaged in a number of other activities, first and foremost in the work of preparing the consortium on research in Workplace Learning under the new Learning Lab Denmark, which formally started up on 1 September 2001 with me as research leader. In fact, one day in August my writing was interrupted in the middle of a sentence and for more than a year I was not able to return to it.

Naturally, I found this extremely frustrating, but I had more than enough to do and, besides, there was not much to be done about it. On the contrary, the possibility of continuing my work on the book seemed more and more remote as time passed.

Then, one day in summer 2002 Hans Siggaard Jensen, director of research at Learning Lab, phoned me to discuss an expansion of my association with the Lab – an association that I was maintaining alongside my teaching and other functions at Roskilde University. To start with I was not particularly accommodating, and during the conversation mentioned my need for time to continue working on the book. This resulted in an offer to purchase my leave of absence from my remaining obligations at Roskilde University in order for me to complete the book as a Learning Lab publication. This was realised from 1 January 2003.

Therefore, I should, first and foremost, like to thank Learning Lab Denmark and Hans Siggaard Jensen for the crucial part they have played in the genesis of the book. Without their high degree of goodwill it would have taken much longer and perhaps never have been finished.

My thanks also go to my colleagues at the Department of Educational Studies, Roskilde University, and in the Learning Lab consortium, the students at Roskilde University's degree programme in pedagogics and PhD students at the Department's Graduate School in Lifelong Learning for the inspiration I have constantly received in the course of my day-to-day work. Special thanks to the colleagues who have been closest to me in recent years – both professionally and personally: Lars Ulriksen, Vibeke Andersen, Christian Helms Jørgensen, Niels Warring, Annegrethe Ahrenkiel, Noemi Katznelson, and, in particular, Birgitte Simonsen, who has read, corrected and discussed the whole manuscript of the book with me, thus providing the occasion and the inspiration for countless improvements, big and small. Other Danish researchers in the area have also been of great significance for me, in particular Jens Berthelsen, Mads Hermansen and Per Fibæk Laursen.

I would also like to express my thanks to the many participants, teachers and leaders at the various adult education programmes with whom I have been in contact over the past decade and who have given me the concrete basis for large parts of the contents and messages of the book, and the persons and bodies in the Ministry of Education and the National Labour Market Authority who have been involved in and have provided funding for the two large-scale empirical projects mentioned.

Special thanks go to the many non-Danish adult education researchers with whom I have been in contact and who have meant so much for my work, especially Peter Alheit (Göttingen/Germany), Ari Antikainen (Joensuu/Finland), Chris Argyris (Harvard/USA), Frank Blackler (Lancaster/UK), David Boud (Sydney/Australia), Stephen Brookfield (Minneapolis/USA), Frank Coffield (London/UK), Per-Erik Ellström (Linköping/Sweden), Yrjö Engeström (Helsinki/Finland), Phil Hodkinson (Leeds/UK), Peter Jarvis (Surrey/UK), Michael Law (Hamilton/NZ), Thomas Leithäuser (Bremen/Germany), Victoria Marsick (New York-/USA), Sharan Merriam (Georgia/USA), Jack Mezirow (New York-/USA), Kjell Rubenson (Vancouver/Canada), Peter Sawchuk (Toronto/Canada), Joyce Stalker (Hamilton/NZ), Robin Usher (Melbourne-/Australia), Ruud van der Veen (New York/USA), Susan Weil (Bristol-/UK), Etienne Wenger (North St. Juan/USA), Danny Wildemeersch (Leuven/Belgium) and Helena Worthen (Chicago/USA).

Finally, thanks to Vibeke Lihn at Roskilde University and Thomas Bestle of Roskilde University Press for their great contribution to the practical design and swift production of the book.

The book was translated by Margaret Malone, whom I thank for close and thorough cooperation. In relation to the Danish version, a section about current Danish adult education policy has been omitted, and a chapter has been added on project work, which is a less well-known pattern of work in adult education outside Scandinavia. In addition, throughout the book a number of references to Danish conditions and literature have been removed and some more references to the international debate and English-language literature have been inserted.

Roskilde, February 2004

Knud Illeris

The Author

Knud Illeris is a well-known figure in the field of educational research and debate in the Scandinavian countries. He holds a PhD in psychology from Copenhagen University and is Professor of Educational Research at Roskilde University, which in 1972 was the first university in the world to base studies mainly on project work. Since 2001 he has also been Research Leader at The Learning Lab Denmark Consortium for Research in Workplace Learning, and in January 2004 he was appointed Honorary Adjunct Professor of Adult Learning and Leadership at Teachers College, Columbia University, New York. Knud Illeris is the author, co-author or editor of more than 70 books and 300 articles on subjects such as learning and motivation, educational planning and practice, project studies, theory of qualification and vocational training, workplace learning, and adult and youth education from the perspective of the learners.

Part 1

Adult education – a societal function

Part 1 of the book deals with adult education as a societal function, i.e. the role, location, conditions and importance of the education programmes in the society, as part of the foundation for the subsequent treatment of the design and practice of these programmes.

Following the introductory chapter about the intentions of the book, its subject areas and structure, the point of departure will be taken in the international slogan about lifelong learning, which in the past decade has been the dominant ideological basis for the upgrading and development of adult education. The ideology implies that development is necessary in consideration of targets concerning economic growth and international competitiveness, the democratic functions of society and social balance, and for the quality of life of members of society. However, in practice there is a clear tendency for economic considerations being unilaterally prioritised.

In the next chapter, the concrete and material basis of adult education programmes and their development and design are addressed. Since the 1960s the development of certain knowledge, skills and qualifications was the topic of discussion, but to a gradually increasing degree the stress has been on general skills, and since the middle of the 1990s the concept of competence development has taken centre stage, not least on the basis of a perception that it is precisely the competencies of members of society that are decisive for society's continued economic development.

Then follows a chapter on current policy in the field of adult education, which in recent years has been dominated by an encounter between trends towards upgrading and trends in the direction of restructuring, savings and increased user payment. At the same time, a tendency towards increased emphasis on the vocationally oriented elements of the education programmes has become more and more dominant.

Finally, the last chapter of part 1 deals with adult education from the perspective of the participants. The lack of this perspective in the general policy for the area is seen as the background for the existing education programmes not adequately meeting the needs of the participants and

thus not leading to the desired development of competence. As a supplement to the official competence thinking, a concept is therefore presented and developed on the ability to resist as a possibility for maintaining
and updating the element of popular character and liberating potential on
which the adult education programmes have traditionally been based.

1. Introduction

This brief introductory chapter summarises the foundation, point of departure and intentions of the book. Demarcating definitions are given of what here is regarded as adult education, adult learning and what in general it is to be adult. Finally, a brief overview is provided of the structure of the book and the main elements of its contents.

1.1. Adult education, society and participants

During the 1990s, matters concerning adult education developed and changed radically in many of the economically prosperous countries. On the one hand, there was a considerable increase in the number of adults taking part in different types of education programmes, and on the other hand, politically, adult education became a matter for labour market policy and thereby also an integrated element of the economic flow of society in a completely new way.

Adult education has become a highly prioritised political area. This was most clearly signalled in the United Kingdom with Tony Blair's famous statement when he came into office as Prime Minister in 1997: *"education, education and education"*, as the three most important areas of social policy. The trend is absolutely clear: education in general and adult education in particular have become central factors in society, economically, politically and culturally.

The same trend has also led to growing educational and research interest in the field, and the number of articles and books about different issues and problems in connection with adult education have radically increased in recent years. This book is an attempt to provide a summarising account of a number of key matters within the area. The main emphasis is that it is a matter of education of *adults* - in contrast to children and young people and thus also the stress is on the participants' situation, experiences and benefit in adult education, and how their needs and interests can be met.

Inherent in this is the fundamental view that the societal functions and significance of adult education programmes are crucially dependent on the way in which they are implemented in practice and are experienced by the participants. At political level there is no lack of fine words about the importance and mission of adult education, while sometimes an understanding of what really takes place in the everyday routines of adult education for the ordinary participants and its impact on them can lag far behind. It is not enough merely to have the largest possible number of participants and keep expenses as low as feasible. At least as decisive is the way in which these participants are recruited, their reactions to being recruited, the academic content, the manner in which instruction takes place, how monitoring and evaluation are carried out etc.

The research and development projects on adult education that I have been involved in during the past 10-15 years have convincingly shown that from the point of view of the participants adult education programmes are at present full of grave problems. The participants often feel objectivised and placed under tutelage in a system that is increasingly being experienced as encroaching. Many resources are wasted in this way, resources that could be put to better use if "the system" had been more aware of the participants, who they are, their needs, and what the education means to them.

Learning and competence development are not mechanical functions that can be regulated on the basis of economic, legal and administrative rationales and decisions alone. It is also a matter of adult, capable people who, in a society that wants to call itself democratic, must be entitled to a considerable degree of co-decision concerning their situation and cannot simply be treated as pupils. This is ethically indefensible and from the point of view of learning – and thus also economically – unwise. Quite naturally there must be some frames regulating adult education programmes on the basis of societal objectives and perspectives and ensuring that the resources are utilised responsibly and appropriately. This is also clearly in the participants' interest. But it implies precisely that the participants have as much co-influence as possible and that they are regarded and treated as adult, responsible people.

1.2. The point of departure and intentions of the book

The point of departure of this book is thus that in the context of adult education it is quite decisive to understand and work on the basis of the fact that it is adults we are talking about, who both qualitatively and quantitatively learn best when they are accepted and treated as adult, capable and responsible in relation to all aspects of the education, from the preceding counselling and referral, to the choice of educational line, academic content and forms of work, to monitoring and evaluation. On the basis of this fundamental position, I try to combine three different intentions in this book:

Firstly, my intention is to draw an adequate *holistic* picture of adult education and adult learning today, thus providing an overview of what the subject encompasses, from the general and supranational political and ideological level, over questions and fundamental views concerning adult learning and competence development, to the different aspects of the design of the education programmes and daily practice at ground-floor level.

Secondly, it is my intention that the book should provide a *professionally and scientifically founded* contribution to the understanding of key matters, contexts and problems within the field. A great deal of psychological, educational, didactic and sociological theory that is part of the fundament, self-perception and practice of adult education, either directly or indirectly, has been adapted on the basis of research on children and young people. It will be a feature of this book to focus on the fact that we are speaking about adults, and in many contexts there will be an examination of the implications of this in relation to current, late modern, globalised market society.

Thirdly and finally, it is my intention to communicate a *message* about adult education and adult learning, a message that has emerged from my respect for and empathy with the participants and their situation in relation to current demands for continued learning and competence development. The book is thus normative in the sense that I cannot imagine that even the best academically underpinned stances can have the character of value-free and objective science. On the contrary, I freely acknowledge that there are matters connected with adult education and adult learning today that I find both ethically unacceptable and inappropriate from the point of view of learning, and this book represents my intention to contribute to a debate about these matters which could hopefully help to change them in the direction of something better, from the perspective of both society and the participants.

It is my hope that the book will function as a broad academic contribution and an intervention that can create debate about the present situation and practice of adult education and adult learning.

1.3. The subject area of the book

It is also important to clarify what is here understood by adult learning and adult education and what it actually means to be an adult.

In general, adult learning has to do with the way in which adult persons in the society of today learn. By learning I understand any change of a permanent nature in the learner's rational, bodily, emotional and social capacity that is not due to biological development, ageing or injury, also including concepts such as socialisation, qualification, personal development and competence development (cf. Illeris 2002, p. 14ff). And by adult I fundamentally understand the psychological fact that the learner regards her/himself and functions as an independent, self-regulating, capable and responsible individual. And more practically in relation to education, by adult I understand that the learners do not themselves regard the education as part of their personal qualification that begins with childhood schooling and, sometimes with breaks, continues until they enter working life and/or family life, or in some other way regard themselves as being out of the school and education system. Thus the condition for speaking about adult learning is dual: the learner must be both psychologically adult and have come past the introductory educational phase of the life cycle.

In accordance with this, adult education is primarily defined as education courses for participants who have emerged from their introductory period of qualification and who in some way or other return to an institutionalised education or training programme. Inherent in this is that the ordinary short-cycle, medium-cycle and long-cycle further education programmes are not part of the book's concept of adult education, irrespective of how adult the participants might be. In addition, supplementary education at academic level is not included, partly because it has not formed part of the empiricism on which the book is based and partly because to a certain extent it is different in nature from the "broad" adult education programmes that the book primarily addresses.

1.4. The structure of the book

On the basis of the above, I have chosen to structure the book in accordance with the way that I perceive adult education programmes as a field of practice with a double point of departure: on the one hand, in their societal location, background and functions, and on the other hand, in the participants, their learning options, life situation and interests. On this basis, the remainder of the book is divided into four main sections.

Part 1 covers chapters 1-5 and deals with the social conditions for adult education, including the ideology concerning lifelong learning, the competency demands of modernity and current adult education policy, and finally a critical discussion of the placing and perspectives of adult education.

Part 2, chapters 6-10, deals with learning, the learning processes and competence development of adults, their learning interests and relation to educating themselves, and the different contexts of which their learning forms a part.

Part 3, covering chapters 11-15, discusses a number of issues having to do with the foundation, objectives and frames of the education and training programmes, their organisation and implementation, and the counselling conducted before and during the study programmes. The chapters take up the topics that are typically included in the area of pedagogy and teaching theory. But this part does not include detailed practical recommendations, because very great differences exist between the different education programmes with respect to their aims, content and participants, and thus also in the concrete design of the more general educational principles and guidelines required.

Finally, part 4 sums up and rounds off of the contents and positions of the book.

2. The ideology of lifelong learning

This chapter deals with the general societal conditions to do with adult educa-tion as they are manifested at ideological level, i.e. the justifications for the poli-cy that is pursued in the area. The concept of "lifelong education" and later the concept of "lifelong learning" have become increasingly more central since adult education began to break the boundaries of traditional popular enlightenment during the economic boom of the 1960s. Adult education has become an in-creasingly more important area for the economic circulation of society, econo-mic growth and international competition, and this has naturally left its mark at political level, not least in supranational organisations such as UNESCO, the OECD, the EU and the World Bank. Today this would seem to have led to tension between the ideals expressed about adults' need for and right to educa-tion on the one hand, and on the other hand actual policy that for by far the greatest part is based on economic and labour-market considerations.

2.1. The political investment in adult education

On the general political level, it is characteristic that traditional concepts such as adult education and popular enlightenment have in recent years been strongly overshadowed by the slogan about "lifelong learning". Such a shift in linguistic usage is hardly a coincidence. When one exami-nes it a little more closely, the development of the concepts of lifelong education and lifelong learning also have a lot to tell about what has ta-ken place in the political arena during the last 30 to 40 years concerning the perception and handling of learning and education options for adults.

On the face of it, lifelong learning would appear to be a harmonious slogan with a progressive and democratic stamp. It is linked to learning as something positive and empowering to which we all should have access during the whole of our lives, and it is simultaneously associated with something which we all are familiar with, because it is actually the case that if one has not suffered severe brain damage, one cannot help learning throughout one's whole life. Inherent in the slogan is also a kind of pro-mise that society will further and support this tendency to learn something new, this specifically human ability to continued lifelong development through learning, which is far wider in scope than what any other living being can attain.

In Denmark the slogan also fits neatly in with the tradition of popular enlightenment and adult education that has roots far back in our history, and which since the start of the folk high school movement in the middle of the 19th century has become deeply embedded in our national self-esteem and self-perception (cf. e.g. Korsgaard 1997). Together with the other Nordic countries, we have always been at the top of international statistics for participation in adult education (cf. e.g. Rubenson 2003, CEDEFOP 2003, p. 18), and that is something with which we are quite content.

However, over the past decade investment in adult education has become a key political issue in almost all technologically and economically highly developed countries and in the so-called transition economies (World Bank 2003). The slogan about lifelong learning has emerged internationally as a part of this development. But it does not merely refer to increased investment. To a high degree it also has to do with the change in the societal importance of adult education programmes that has taken place in extension of the economic boom of the 1960s.

At that time, the development of society with far-reaching technological breakthroughs, a sharp rise in productivity, the lack of skilled labour, the many women who entered the labour market, and the expansion of basic and youth education created a radically increased need to upgrade the qualifications of the adult workforce. In a number of countries, this led inter alia to the further expansion of vocationally oriented adult education programmes, and by degrees there was considerable growth in general adult education.

While the direct reason for the expansion of adult education was thus clearly economic and labour market oriented in nature, the ideology that found expression in the slogans about lifelong education and lifelong learning was far broader and more humanistic in orientation. When the slogans appear in official documents they by no means overlook the labour-market perspective, but traditionally the main emphasis has been the general cultural and social development of the potential of adults in step with the increased possibilities created by the economy. At the same time lifelong education and learning have been regarded as a means of building bridges across the educational gulf between different population groups and generations.

2.2. The ideal of lifelong learning

The thematisation of the concept of lifelong learning started in the International Labour Organisation (ILO) during the 1960s (Lassen 2000, p. 61), but the decisive ideological breakthrough for this international orientation came in 1972 with the report of the United Nations Educational, Scientific and Cultural Organization (UNESCO) report: "Learning to be" – edited by Edgar Faure, who had earlier been both Minister for Education and Prime Minister in France (Faure et al. 1972). The report paints, convincingly and with a great deal of pathos, the necessity of a thorough, world-wide educational reform:

> "Wherever we find a traditional educational system which has stood the test of time and was generally thought to need no more than a few occasional minor improvements, a few more or less automatic adjustments, it is currently unleashing an avalanche of criticisms and suggestions which often go so far as to question it in its entirety. [...] The aim of education is to enable man to be himself, to 'become himself'. And the aim of education in relation to employment and economic progress should be not so much to prepare young people and adults for a specific, lifetime vocation, as to 'optimise' mobility among the professions and afford a permanent stimulus to the desire to learn and to train one-self. In brief, without abandoning the expansion of education, its objectives, methods and structures should be thoroughly reappraised." (Faure et al. 1972, pp. xix and xxxi-xxxii).

At that period, attitudes to lifelong education were in general very idealistic and humanistic. They basically were that the rising welfare of societies should also be used to improve the possibilities that the members of society had for personal and cultural enrichment and empowerment by means of continued education and development. This was the central thrust in what the Swedish-Canadian educational researcher Kjell Rubenson has called the utopian-humanistic phase of the movement, which lasted until the middle of the 1980s (Rubenson 2004).

2.3. From lifelong education to lifelong learning

However, as a number of countries actually saw a significant increase in the number of students flocking to adult education programmes that extended beyond the traditional general learning area, they also saw rising consumption of resources and an increased contribution to the qualification of the workforce, and thereby it became increasingly relevant to include economic arguments in the area. It is characteristic that around the same time, OECD, which is the international body entrusted with the promotion of the relatively affluent member countries' economic development, increasingly assumed the leading role in the area instead of the broader and more generally oriented UNESCO. Rubenson (2004) calls it the economist phase from the mid-1980s up to the middle of the 1990s.

At the beginning of the 1990s, the term "education" was also gradually replaced with "learning", due to a growing recognition that the decisive factor is not what is produced by formalised education, but what is *learned* through any form of activity (cf. Illeris 2002, chapter 1) – but perhaps at the same time also due to an incipient understanding that a comprehensive institutionalisation of adult education could become a hugely costly undertaking (cf. Field 2002, p. 21ff). In any event this shift in terminology took place in parallel with a rapidly rising interest in concepts like "practice learning" and "workplace learning", even though the overall state control of education and labour market policy has clearly found it difficult to figure out how to relate to non-institutionalised learning.

An important milestone was the publication in 1996 of the OECD report "Lifelong learning for all" (OECD 1996). The OECD report was published subsequent to a meeting of the ministers of education of the OECD member countries, a bulky tome of 340 large double-column pages full of tables and figures. Most of the report is concerned with demonstrating the necessity of making a focused effort in the field of adult education, and discussions of how this effort might be implemented, financed and administered. However, not least the initial part, made up of the issues for discussion for the meeting and the ministers' communiqué, may be considered perhaps the most apt official expression of the political-economic *ideology* of lifelong learning, which was at that time well on its way to replacing the old humanist-idealist approach.

It is important here first to notice that the slogan on this occasion was augmented with the addition "for all". In this lies partly a message that a wide scope of the effort is considered of decisive importance, and at the same time a proclaimed counter-action against the well-known tendency that efforts in the field of adult education perpetuate the social imbalances of primary education, so that the already well-educated are upgraded further, while those with brief schooling participate to a considerably lower extent.

This broad and socially oriented fundamental attitude is a general characteristic of the report, which is built around the view that the concept of lifelong learning contains, and unfolds through, three integrated perspectives which the effort must cover and unite, that is, personal development, economic growth and social cohesion. This is the formulation used at the start of the education ministers' communiqué with the chairman's words:

> "We are all convinced of the crucial importance of learning throughout life for enriching personal lives, fostering economic growth and maintaining social cohesion." (OECD 1996, p. 21).

The idea of personal development is characterised in the report by including two inseparable dimensions, that is, respectively the academic and vocational qualifications and the more personal competences (the relationship between qualifications and competences is considered in more detail in chapter 3 of this book). Even though both are considered absolutely necessary, the main emphasis is clearly placed on the personal competences. The issues for discussion thus highlight that abilities such as creativity, initiative and responsiveness are necessary as prerequisites for self-expression, higher earnings and employment and for innovation and productivity (OECD 1996, p. 15). Special attention is paid to the concept of "learning-to-learn skills", which is described as

> *"the ability to find information and to extract the relevant from the less relevant, to relate it to previously acquired knowledge, to contextualise it, and put it to use again, as needed." (OECD 1996, p.105)*

Through this concept the authors also make the link to primary education by emphasising that lifelong learning comprises the entire course of a person's life, and basic education and adult education must be viewed in context.

With respect to the notion of economic growth, it is concerned with the economic progress of the individual, of enterprises and of society, and the three levels are seen as interconnected and dependent. Hence lifelong learning at the individual level is of decisive importance for both companies and society, and the highway to the economic growth of companies and society goes through the lifelong learning of individuals:

> *"the question is not whether OECD countries can pay the price for lifelong learning, but whether they can afford not to." (OECD 1996, p. 87)*

The report makes no particular effort to conceal that the aim of the entire exercise is economic growth; the OECD is after all, as mentioned, an organisation which is to represent and promote the economic interests of its member countries. However, the concept of lifelong learning highlights the dependence of the economies of nations and corporations on the level of qualifications possessed by its citizens and employees, which again means that society, companies and the individual run the risk of being left behind if lifelong learning fails to take place. The notion of economic growth thus finds expression not only at the macroeconomic, or national economic, level, but is seen as inextricably bound up with the corporate and individual level, although no explicit passage attempts to provide documentation to that effect.

The notion of social cohesion has, in connection with lifelong learning, again two dimensions. One dimension is that lifelong learning can contribute to underpinning and strengthening democracy. The other is that lifelong learning can counteract social exclusion. Both dimensions contain the notion that in order to keep pace with modern society and contribute to the appropriate function of modern society, lifelong learning will be a necessity.

2.4. Neo-liberal ideology

The OECD report from 1996 thus became, at one and the same time, the end of the economist phase and the beginning of what Rubenson (2004) terms as the neo-liberal phase, which is characterised by being more ideological, that is, that the argumentation assumes more of the character of attitude, while there is actually a slow-down in the use of government resources in the area (cf. also chapter 4).

Seen from this perspective, it is probably no coincidence that gradually and increasingly in Europe it was the EU that, as a third supranational forum, took over the vanguard as concerns the promotion and coordination of its Member States' policy in this area. This was done with, among other things, a memorandum from the EU Commission that was published in 2000 and which, far more directly action-oriented than the OECD report, calls for concrete political initiatives:

> *"Its purpose is to* launch a European-wide debate *on a comprehensive strategy for implementing lifelong learning at individual and institutional levels, and in all spheres of public and private life." (Commission of the European Communities 2000, p. 3).*

Compared to the OECD report it is thus conspicuous that the EU memorandum to a far higher degree emphasised the significance of non-institutionalised learning:

> "Lifelong learning *is no longer just one aspect of education and training; it* must become the guiding principle *for provision and participation across the full continuum of learning contexts." (Commission of the European Communities 2000, p. 3)*

At the same time, the memorandum maintains the balance between the personal and the societal aim as it states

> *"two equally important aims for lifelong learning: promoting active citizenship and promoting employability. [...] Both employability and active citizenship are dependent upon having adequate and up-to-date knowledge and skills to take part in and make a contribution to economic and social life."* (Commission of the European Communities 2000, p. 5)

However, the most important thing is without doubt that the memorandum, and the procedures it determined, very clearly aimed at committing the EU Member States to the implementation of far-reaching structural reforms with a view to actually arriving at radical improvements of the conditions for lifelong learning for all being promoted.

The most recent new development in the area is that yet another supranational organisation, i.e. the World Bank, has forcefully entered the debate with a view to promoting lifelong learning (The World Bank, 2003). First, this has produced the sympathetic perspective that the overwhelmingly predominant focus is no longer on the technologically and economically well-developed countries, but that also the so-called transition countries and the developing countries as such are strongly included, both in the debate and in concrete initiatives. At the same time, the argumentation of the World Bank is unequivocal, with no ideological and humanistically oriented evasion: the aim is, in brief and clear terms,

> *"creating a labor force able to compete in the global economy."* (World Bank 2003, p. xviii)

Unfortunately, the argumentation in the World Bank's contribution is, however, economist and simplifying in a way which is so naive and devoid of human understanding that administrative and pedagogical professionals in the area consider it both unprofessional and untenable. For instance the English professor of education research Frank Coffield, who for many years has been chairman of the Learning Society Research Programme initiated by the UK Economic and Social Research Council, "the learning society", considers the World Bank' s model of lifelong learning "an incomplete farrago of ill-understood theories of learning", and Coffield speaks, in this connection, furthermore of "the international, cliché-ridden rhetoric in which lifelong learning has been entrapped and which is produced by such organisations as OECD, UNESCO and ... the World Bank", a rhetoric that is "vague" in a way that makes it "useful to politicians, who can subtly change their interpretation of the term as their policies bob and weave in response to economic upturns and downturns" and makes "people like me ... equate lifelong learning with social control" (Coffield 2003, p. 42 and 40).

Unfortunately, criticism such as this today finds rich soil to a significant degree. It has long been apparent that lifelong learning must be understood as an ideological slogan, but to many it has had a positive and rallying aim which, however, it has become increasingly difficult to maintain.

2.5. Lifelong learning in the tension field between ideology and economy

I have opened the consideration of the societal foundations of adult education with a summary review of the concepts of lifelong education and lifelong learning, because it is important to understand the character of the political-ideological definition generally referred to.

The first matter that is conspicuous is that this definition for more than 40 years has first and foremost been borne and developed by supranational organisations. Thereby it has, not least at the level of national policy and administration in the ministries involved, assumed a special character of a sort of indisputable truth or manifest destiny. At the beginning these initiatives appeared remote and idealistic, something to be celebrated in after-dinner speeches, and which progressive forces could refer to when they wanted to plead for reforms. However, since the mid 1990s, they have assumed an increasingly urgent and inevitable character: this is the way these matters must be understood and this is the way in which they must be realised in practical policy.

Another significant matter is that the argumentation covers a wide field all the time. The notion of lifelong learning as ideology is legitimised in a decisive way when the wordings emphasise a conjunction of the societal and the individual level. One might perhaps on the face of it believe that the interest in economic growth relates to the societal level, the personal development dimension to the individual level, and the social cohesion to a kind of bridging. However, this is not the way it is presented. On the contrary, it is highly characteristic that in all three dimensions it is emphasised that both levels form part of and are integrated, conjoined to a high degree with working life and companies as the link. Both individuals and society need a combination of personal development, economic growth and social cohesion.

Thereby the ideology is, however, also one of the most coherent, and exactly therefore also one of the most opaque, manifestations of the late-modern so-called neo-liberal economic, political and cultural modes of perception which denies the societal disparities and postulates that what is good for society, i.e. fundamentally maximised economic growth, is good for everybody. Therein lies a tendency to disregard the fact that economic growth is often gained at somebody's expense, both in the national and the international distribution of goods, and, at the same time, is often based on short-term interests that may involve great long-term costs, as is, for instance, the case when the earth's resources are overexploited and when pollution and health concerns receive low priority.

This also applies to a great extent to the area of education and learning, and in connection with lifelong learning the issues to a high degree increasingly depend on what the small addition "for all" is in reality intended to communicate and in how it is realised. As will appear later in this book, great and grave issues spring from these matters, and the problems are not merely a question of distribution. Actually the supranational texts are quite explicit about the necessity of giving priority to those who are poorest in economic, social and educational terms. However, it remains a central issue whether these measures are sufficient and are being implemented in a way that is relevant seen from the life-situation and perspectives of these participants. The fact that this question is becoming so urgent is probably due to the possibility that there may be deficient understanding of fundamental societal differences and disparities in the point of departure.

If the most vulnerable in our society are to commit themselves effectively in education and learning, it must take place on their own terms and be concerned with something that makes sense from their own perspective. In Denmark the so-called "day high schools" (not be confused with the folk high schools, because they are not boarding schools and the intention is to give people on the verge of social marginalisation a chance for a new start), constitute one of the areas of the education system that most clearly has tried to establish solidarity with the weakest on their own terms. However, the political establishment has not seen this as sufficiently goal-directed (in relation to vocationally oriented activation), and therefore the day high schools now experience such poor financial circumstances that many have had to close down and the remaining are so involved in a constant struggle for survival that it easily affects the quality of their work.

Seen with Danish eyes, it has been the obvious approach to view the ideology of lifelong learning as a modernised version of our national heritage from the high schools and general education. Not least former Social Liberal Minister for Education, Ole Vig Jensen, had this perspective on the matter. The introduction to the Danish version of the OECD report thus states that

> "the solution proposed by the Ministers of Education is lifelong learning or lifelong education. The 26 OECD member countries agree on this. [...] Lifelong education should not merely be regarded as necessary for the economic development of society. Lifelong educationt must also contain general elements – which was emphasised at the meeting by, among others, Ole Vig Jensen [the then Danish Minister for Education]. This is not to play down the importance of satisfying the requirements of trade and industry by means of goal-directed educational activities, but to point out the importance of lifelong education for the individual person, for social cohesion, and for the maintenance and development of democracy in the member countries." (Danish Ministry of Education, 1996, p. 1)

To all appearances it is the other member countries that have now joined what we have been accustomed to perceiving as the Danish model. And it is precisely the broad, popular and democratic perspective in Denmark that has been praised with indefatigable energy alongside the social and economic dimension and the interests of business.

However, currently the development seems to be moving in another direction, both in Denmark and internationally. In the words of John Field, who is England's first professor of lifelong learning, and who declares himself "a shameless advocate of lifelong learning":

> "Yet when subjected to closer inspection, much of the policy interest in lifelong learning is in fact preoccupied with the development of a more productive and efficient workforce. The [British Ministry of Education] white paper's agenda is driven primarily by a desire to raise the nation's economic competitiveness and improve its standard of living, defined in largely material terms [...] Indeed, to some extent lifelong learning has been used by policy makers as little more than a modish repackaging of rather conventional policies for post-16 education and training, with little that is new or innovative." (Field 2002, p. viii-ix)

Another internationally known English researcher who has been strongly involved in the movement for lifelong learning, education sociologist Peter Jarvis, has also seen this dichotomy. In his presentation at the international conference on lifelong learning that was held in connection with Denmark's EU Presidency in the second half of 2002, he said, among other things:

> "Lifelong learning was [in the most recent official EU document] defined as 'all learning activity throughout life whether it is in formal, non-formal or informal situations. In a real sense this approach seeks to recapture the concept of lifelong learning since it has been usurped by the economic and vocational emphasis placed upon it in recent years. [...] The argument of this paper is that the tension between global capitalism and the aspirations of those who endeavour to put these lifelong learning policies into practice is insufficiently recognized." (Jarvis 2002, p. 3)

Lifelong learning is, in its point of departure, a both ideal and necessary slogan. Actually, incredibly many of the formulations and reflections found in the many official texts from both UNESCO, the OECD and the EU contain profound insights and fine intentions for a better life for all, and learning is in its essence characterised by pleasure, enriching and liberating (cf. Furth 1987). However, studies in real life adult education show with great clarity that this is not always the actual experience. In the following chapters I shall repeatedly return to this dichotomy, its causes, and my suggestions for ways to counteract it.

However beautiful the intentions and idealistic and ideological formulations might be, they have only limited impact, as appears from the quotation from Jarvis above, whereas the real economic and power structures, and the material relations that govern them, wield truly massive influence. I shall return to this in the next chapter.

3. The competence demands of modernity

This chapter deals on a general level with the more concrete or material societal requirements towards which adult education today must orient itself, i.e. the types of qualifications and competences demanded by working life and adult life in general. These demands range from the more traditional professional qualifications to modern personal and social competences, and as a central point they imply that one must be flexible and ready for change in order to be in a position to manage new conditions and situations. There is a great deal of uncertainty as to the way in which such qualification or development of competence is to take place in practice, but on the general level both national and supranational authorities are working to clarify these matters and translate them into understandings and models that, inter alia, can guide the development of adult education programmes. Simultaneously, at many educational institutions and in working life experiments are under way in an attempt to find new paths vis-à-vis the new challenges. The chapter provides an overview of these complex matters, which are of great importance for the current development and design of adult education programmes.

3.1. Disciplining for flexibility

The previous chapter focused on the ideological basis for adult education and the concept of lifelong learning. However, since the 1970s it has often been demonstrated and discussed that the societal basis for the development of the school- and education systems must not primarily be sought in ideological arguments. These arguments may best be viewed as legitimisation while the decisive basis lies in the functions which the education programmes carry out in maintaining and developing society. It has been pointed out that the central societal function schools and education programmes are concerned with is providing the qualifications that are necessary for society to be able to function and develop within the framework of the existing economic and power structures (cf. e.g. Huisken 1972, Masuch 1972).

Furthermore, schools and education programmes, in addition to qualification, also take care of a number of other functions in society, including socialisation, social sorting, legitimisation and storing, besides the self-maintenance function which later was pointed out as a significant factor for the understanding of the ways in which different organisations function.

The summarising headline for the fundamental function in society of schools and education is "disciplining for wage labour", understood in the sense that the development of the entire education system has taken place in step with the development of wage labour as the dominant working relation. It is also understood that wage labour, besides various professional qualifications more generally, has presumed general acceptance of this relation, i.e. that one sells oneself as labour on a labour market within given timeframes, where the buyer (the employer) has the right to manage and distribute work, i.e. to decide on the use to which the labour is put. The point is thus quite fundamentally that society's members agree, as a matter of course, to accept and loyally carry out work determined by another within certain hours, and this is of course precisely what is generally being taught and trained in schools and education programmes.

This perception has, I suppose, still validity at an elementary level, but at the same time it has over the years been overlaid by some developments in working life that on the one hand presume such a fundamental "wage-earner consciousness", but at the same time place the main emphasis on the ability and willingness to adapt to keep up with the rapid development of work caused by, i.a. the conditions imposed by the technological development, globalisation and the market society. Disciplining for wage labour has developed into a paradox-filled underlying demand for "disciplining for flexibility".

3.2. The development in qualification requirements

In the so-called General Qualification Project, which was carried out by the Adult Education Research Group at Roskilde University 1992-97 (Andersen et al. 1994, 1996), a thorough report was conducted of the development in the qualification requirements, qualification theories and qualification analyses from the first American contributions at the end of the 1950s, and later through German and Danish contributions, in particular.

Already in the first major German study of the qualification requirements in the industrial area, it was demonstrated as decisive that work not only makes demands for qualifications of a professional and technical character, but also some more general and personality-related requirements, and the research distinguished between the "process-dependent" qualifications, which relate directly to certain work processes, and the broader "process-independent qualifications", which consist of general skills, perception modes and abilities that have the character of general preconditions for many different work processes (Kern & Schumann 1970).

If we follow the course of the research as it develops, it is characteristic that it is these process-independent, broad or general qualifications which increasingly attract attention and are ascribed significance, and at the same time things slide in a direction which means that within these qualifications there is increasing emphasis on the personal characteristics, such as e.g. typically independence, responsibility, flexibility, the ability to co-operate and the ability for analytical reasoning.

More generally we are seeing increasing understanding that qualifications cannot be understood and developed independently of the subjectivity of the individual, i.e. how the individual perceives her or himself in relation to society and forms part of society's different relations. Both in education and work we play a part as subjects, we perceive activities on the basis of our own identity and situation, and this unavoidably influences everything we experience, learn, think and do.

A mechanical perception of qualifications that overlooks these aspects will eventually always fail. Attempts to develop or practise qualifications while bypassing subjectivity will at best achieve exterior and inflexible tools that are used without commitment and reflection. They might have some justification in connection with entirely routine work processes, but in a modern working life, which strives for continual development and movement, independence, cooperation and service-orientation, they are no use.

Naturally there is still a need for technical and professional qualifications, and in some areas, such as information technology and foreign languages, these needs are even rising steeply. However, it is at the same time characteristic that such qualifications in their practical application to a growing degree form part of a integrated interplay with personal abilities and become more or less useless without this interplay: a contrary and inflexible specialist is not in much demand these days.

This gives some educational problems because traditionally the education programmes have predominantly aimed at mediating professional or academic skills content. Now the interplay between the academic and the personal aspects becomes increasingly crucial, and this requires the development of forms of education which the institutions and the systems are not immediately willing to accept, and which most teachers are quite insecure towards, if not downright hostile.

3.3. A qualification theoretical model

In extension of these realisations the General Qualification Project developed a search model concerned with the "subjectivity in a qualification perspective", i.e. how subjectivity or "societal consciousness" may appropriately be perceived in connection with activities in which focused qualification is the entire or partial aim (see Andersen et al 1994).

The model consists of two figures, which we have named the "Tulip" and the "Map", respectively. The "Tulip" includes as two petals the two life-spheres: "working life" and "social life". The two life-spheres are, as concerns qualifications, fundamentally different because the qualifications in the two spheres are assessed according to fundamentally different rationales. In working life we basically assess qualifications according to their utility value, i.e. what pays. In social life outside work we assess qualifications according to their practicality, i.e. what is good, appropriate or satisfying.

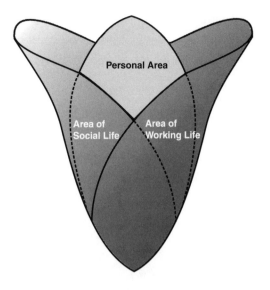

Figure 1: Subjectivity viewed in the perspective of qualification: The "Tulip"– the three areas of the search model

This means that qualifications developed in one area cannot immediately be used or have the same character when we enter into another area. At a factory we saw e.g. how women with great competence in managing and organising their household and family life neither wanted nor were able to apply the same organisational qualifications in their working life, even though they were strongly encouraged to do so by management. In working life they wanted to do what they were told without personal decisions and commitment. This was what they were paid for, and their organisational qualifications were reserved for their "free time".

However, there is also a third area in the figure, a core between the two petals, which we have called "the personality". It is concerned with the personal abilities or qualifications that may be developed through both life-spheres, but which the whole time we endeavour to maintain together as a unit or "integrity". Personal qualifications *may* also be developed outside the life-spheres, but this only takes place in special situations in which we are mentally outside these spheres, which e.g. is the aim of therapy.

In the "Map" we must imagine that the tulip has been turned out as a surface (so that the conjoining of the petals "in front of" and "behind" the core are not visible). At the same time, we have introduced a horizontal layering of the tulip's three areas so as to produce nine fields, which are to be understood as nine different subjective areas for qualification. The dotted lines are intended to mark that the fields are not sharply distinguished in relation to each other, and downwards there is a tendency for the fields to grow together because at this level there is a subjective tendency to mental integration.

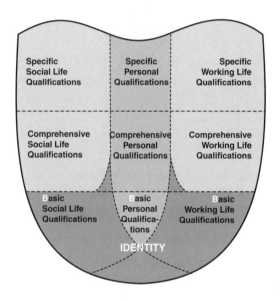

Figure 2: Subjectivity viewed in the perspective of qualification: The "Map" – the nine areas of the search model

We have called the levels of the model the "concrete", the "general" and the "basic" level, respectively. These designations refer to the fact that different types of qualifications have a more or less deep subjective impact on us. The concrete level is concerned with qualifications which typically have the character of practical skills, ready factual knowledge, and similar, which only to a modest extent concern our perception of self. The general level is typically concerned with broader understanding and coherent patterns of action. The basic level, which we also call "identity", is concerned with overarching qualifications or general modes of experience, thought and action that form a direct part of our self-perception.

In this way we "map" subjectivity in nine different areas of relevance for the qualification processes. Different types of activities develop different types of qualifications according to which areas are activated. The limits are not sharp, but are nonetheless of importance for when and how we can and will apply the qualifications, how deep they are rooted in us, and thus how accessible they are to changes and new developments.

The model has two especially important functions. First, it attracts attention to the fact that qualifications always form part of a whole, a subjectivity that has certain specific structures that are developed individually and inevitably influence the qualification: the same influences fit in differently in different individuals and therefore give different results, as any schoolteacher knows. Second, the model signals that there are different types of qualifications, and it attempts to provide a certain overview of their mutual interconnection.

However, the model is, of course, a construction. It is in no way postulated that "consciousness looks like this" or anything to that effect. This is merely a search model, an aid to provide some support for e.g. the development of curricula or the discussion of the different typical qualification profiles of various groups.

In the concluding report from the General Qualification Project we, furthermore, distinguished between qualifications and capacities as two sides of the same coin or two subjective layers in the individual, where the qualifications are concerned with what is "relevant for the societal work with which the individual in question is employed or would be able to work", while capacities are a human's "total ability", i.e. everything which the individual in question is able to handle, irrespective of whether it is relevant for societal work or not" (Illeris et al. 1995, p. 147).

The difference between qualifications and capacities is thus not of a quantitative nature, for any capacity is a potential qualification, and the question of when it also becomes a real qualification is focused on when it becomes relevant for the societal work of the individual in question.

This also means that one could apply precisely the same models, the "Tulip" and the "Map", for the capacities as for the qualifications, because structurally there is no difference. We illustrated this by means of a figure in which two "maps" are placed with an interval which we might call the socially generated field of tension that interjects itself between existence as a human being (which is the framework containing the capacities) and societal work (which is the framework containing the qualifications).

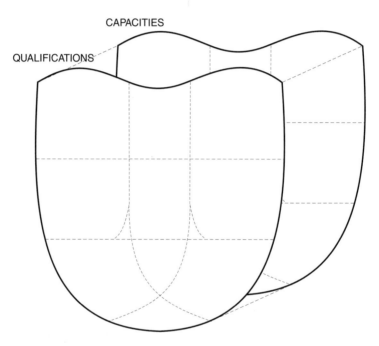

Figure 3: Qualifications and capacities

This distinction between qualifications and capacities may be understood as a precursor of the development of the concept of competences that has taken place meanwhile, and which I shall now consider, because it is of central importance to the understanding of the aim and character of adult education today.

3.4. The new concept of competence

Since the General Qualification Project and the development of the tulip model, there has been a marked shift in the rhetoric concerning the intended outcomes of education programmes. This is concerned first and foremost with the fact that the concept of "qualifications" to a large extent has been replaced with the concept of "competence", and this is neither mere coincidence nor an irrelevant terminological novelty. On the contrary, it might be said that this language change constitutes an attempt to take the full consequence of the development in qualification interest that has been outlined above:

> *"The concept of competence refers [...] to a person's being qualified in a broader sense. It is not merely that the person masters a professional area, but also that the person can apply this professional knowledge - and more than that, apply it in relation to the requirements inherent in a situation which perhaps in addition is uncertain and unpredictable. Thus competence also includes the person's assessments and attitudes, and ability to draw on a considerable part of his/her more personal qualifications." (Jørgensen 1999, p. 4)*

In relation to the above, one might also say that the competence concept endeavours to summarise qualifications and capacities in a perception which is at once concerned with a person's potential and practical performance. Competence is thus a unifying concept that integrates everything it takes in order to perform in a given situation or context. The concrete qualifications are incorporated in the competence rooted in personality, and one may generally also talk of the competence of organisations and nations.

Where the concept of qualifications historically has its point of departure in requirements for specific knowledge and skills, and to an increasing degree has been used for pointing out that this knowledge and these skills have underlying links and roots in personality, the perception in the concept of competence has, so to speak, been turned upside down. In this concept, the point of departure lies at the personal level in relation to certain contexts, and the more specific qualifications are something that can be drawn in and contribute to the realisation of the competence. Where the concept of qualifications took its point of departure in the individual elements, the individual qualifications, and has developed towards a more unified perception, the concept of competence starts with a unity, e.g. the type of person or organisation it takes to solve a task or fulfil a job, and on the basis of this points out any possible different qualifications necessary.

It is thus characteristic that the concept of competence does not, like the concept of qualifications, have its roots in industrial sociology, but in organisational psychology and modern management thinking. It has thus acquired a dimension of "smartness" which makes it easier to "sell" politically, but also makes it tend toward a superficiality which in this context seems to characterise large parts of the management orientation (cf. Argyris 2000); it has thus been called a "prostitute" concept rooted in an economic view of man by the Danish philosopher, Jens Erik Kristensen.

However, at the same time it is difficult to deny that it captures something central in the current situation of learning and qualification. It is ultimately concerned with how a person, an organisation or a nation is able to handle a relevant, but often unforeseen and unpredictable problematic situation, because we know with certainty that late modern development constantly generates new and unknown problems, and the ability to respond openly and in an appropriate way to new problematic situations is crucial in determining who will manage in the globalised market society.

The shift in perspective, which the concept of competence is an expression of, thus includes also the new perception of the relationship between learning and education, where non-institutionalised learning, and not least learning with a direct basis in working life, has come into focus, as was also outlined in the previous chapter concerning the concept of lifelong learning. However, at the same time the concept involves a colossal challenge to the institutionalised education programmes. For how may one develop, in terms of education and in a goal-directed manner, the abilities to handle the known and still unknown problems in an increasingly diverse and incomprehensible world?

Here it is not enough just to point to "practice learning" and "work-place learning", as has been a strong tendency. For there is no avoiding the fact that the school and education system will remain the "government apparatus" that has been erected to be the primary tool of the public sector for providing the socially necessary qualifications, and it will also clearly in future be in both the practical and economic interest of the private and public sectors that the competences to the widest possible extent are developed in employees in advance, without imposing the burden on the economy and the daily work which a far-reaching qualification and competence development in the workplace will involve.

3.5. The concept of competence in practice

It was not very many years ago that competence first and foremost was a formal and legal matter, something one was formally accorded as an authorisation to act (handle cases, make decisions, etc.) in a limited area, in private practice or in the public administration. Since then, however, the concept has spread in the modern sense outlined above, both within the area of education, in working life, and as a management and policy related concept, with great impact. Today there are incredibly many and diverse definitions of what competence is and a lively discussion on the perception and definition of the concept.

An important trend with close relation to both national and international political and administrative organs attempts to define the concept by pointing to a number of central types of competences. In Denmark, a privately established "Competence Council" has thus published its proposal for four so-called "core competences", which each include two to three "indexes":

- *learning competence (professionalism, organisational learning, cross-cultural learning)*
- *change competence (innovation, mobility)*
- *relationship competence (networking, communication, responsibility)*
- *meaning competence (focus, identity)*
  (Schultz 2000, p. 14).

At the official level, a governmental development project has been initiated, which is concerned with the extensive research work that has been carried out in the area for a number of years in the OECD, first in relation to fundamental school education, and since 1997 i.a. in the so-called DeSeCo-project (Definition and Selection of Competences), in which researchers have done extensive work on demonstrating, describing and discussing a number of key competences:

- *Social competencies | Co-operation*
- *Literacies | Intelligent and applicable knowledge*
- *Learning competence | Lifelong learning*
- *Communication competencies*
- *Value orientation*
- *Self-competence | Self-management*
- *Political competence | Democracy*
- *Ecological competence, relationship to Nature*
- *Cultural competencies (Aesthetic, Creativity, Intercultural, Media)*
- *Health, Sports, Physical competence*
  (DeSeCo 2001,pp. 21-28)

Even though DeSeCo's work is carried out with diligent care and with the inclusion of a great number of experts and critics from many countries, there are, in my opinion, some fundamental problems involved in this entire approach.

If one compares the two lists here reproduced, it is clear that they are of a somewhat different character. One goes into some central human functions, the possibilities for creating learning, change, relations and meaning, while the other primarily takes its point of departure in some societal areas where there is a need for members of society to have some competences. The issue is that the entire basis for what it is one is to categorise is unclear, and that it is fundamentally impossible to pose final lists of the human potential, because it is something that is acted out specifically in the interplay between people and their surroundings, which is constantly developing.

The approach therefore fundamentally involves a reduction of what competences consist of in the first place and how they find expression, and this is closely conjoined to the fact that we are essentially not looking at competence development, but at political control and thereby also at social control; or, as it has been formulated by the Danish competence researcher Pia Bramming:

> *"There is a lot of competence, and competence is constantly being developed, because the world is fundamentally changing and competent before anyone wishes to change anything at all. If one finds that there is a shortage of development or competence, it is because one finds that the development ought to be different. However, then one has a control problem, not a competence problem or competence shortage." (Bramming 2003, p. 16)*

The entire notion of drawing up lists of competences springs from the need of authorities for evaluation, measuring and steering instruments. This is of course fundamentally legitimate; we have governments and other authorities because there must of necessity be an administration of society, which is today a highly complicated affair. It is, I suppose, also legitimate that the control is fundamentally exercised in relation to aims for economic growth and international competitiveness, even though such a policy entails some very serious problems.

However, it becomes problematic when the interconnections between the ends and the means are so dubious as is the case here, and much experience shows that the results will be presented, understood and used as though there was not such an enormous uncertainty. It causes concern when control problems are represented as competence problems and the issue is thereby removed from the controlling instances to those who are to be controlled. This may be seen in particular by observing some of the places where people whose competences have been deemed insufficient are to be taught some more marketable competences. I shall return to this later in the book.

3.6. Competence, learning and education

With the modern concept of competence we have succeeded in defining and naming a matter of great importance for society, organisations, companies, the education system and the individual, a matter which both practice and research within the education and working life areas have struggled with for decades.

However, unfortunately, the concept of competence is, in the same way as the concept of lifelong learning, rapidly becoming the horse dragging a carriage of narrow economically oriented control interests that empty the concept of the liberating potential springing from the place of the competences as relevant contemporary mediators between the societal challenges and individual ways of managing them.

The concept of competence is thus central as a point of departure for a more nuanced understanding of what learning in general, and not least the learning processes of adults, is all about today. In such an endeavour, e.g. the models from the General Qualification Project and other realisations from qualification research still have their significance and justification as an approach to building a bridge to a correspondingly modernised learning understanding, with an aim to arriving at theoretically founded and practically tested proposals for how contemporary competence development may be realised for different people in accordance with their possibilities and needs, both within and outside the institutionalised education programmes. Such an approach has, in my opinion, far better and more well-founded possibilities for contributing to real competence development, at the individual level as well as the societal level, than the measuring and comparing approach that has been outlined above. However, it will to a much higher degree be oriented towards experiments and initiatives at practice level than the top-down control approach inherent in the measuring models.

The EU has actually, through the organisation CEDEFOP (European Centre for the Development of Vocational Training), made an effort in this direction, which has i.a. produced a massive volume on "Training and learning for competence" (CEDEFOP 2001). However, the work shows at the same time how difficult it is to handle such issues at a general and international level; it all too easily turns into endless scribbling, with very limited innovation and impact when so many different perceptions and interests are to be collated.

In my opinion, there is more perspective to be found in different professional approaches in the area, although they remain for now rather scattered and preliminary. The Danish social and development psychologist Per Schultz Jorgensen has e.g. proposed that the solution to the issue of competence must be sought in connection with the establishment of "competence developing environments" that constitute a productive framework, prioritise possible courses of action and provide a common understanding of the perspective:

"It is possible that through such an approach a basis for a pedagogical application of the concept of competence might be created, something which the many experiments in this area must clarify. It is an approach which rests on the development of the pedagogical culture, e.g. in schools and a new orientation of this culture in the direction of common understanding of competence as rooted in social integration. [...] The aim is that any skill must be extended by means of accumulating experience, with implementation in an applied context and with assignment of a responsibility that creates the involvement. [...] The key words ... are: (1) skills, (2) experiential knowledge, (3) practical application and (4) own and common responsibility for the process." (Jørgensen 2001, pp. 205-206)

This is merely one among many proposals made in recent years to view schools and educational institutions in a perspective of competence development, and corresponding proposals have also be put forward with regard to competence development in working life.

The main ingredients that keep recurring in various ways in the different professional contributions seem clearly enough to be that competence development may be promoted in environments where qualification development takes place in connection with a (retrospective) actualisation of relevant experience and contexts, that (at the same time) interplay between relevant activities and interpretation of these activities in a theoretical conceptual framework, and a (prospective) reflection and perspective, i.e. a pervasive perspective in relation to the participants' life or biography, linked with a meaning and conception-oriented reflection and a steady alternation between the individual and the social levels within the framework of a community.

This book may i.a. be seen as an attempt to contribute to thinking and understanding of adult education programmes and adult learning in such a perspective.

4. Current adult education policy

While the two previous chapters have dealt with the background to the current development in adult education programmes, this chapter examines the policy that has been pursued in the area in recent years. As a point of departure, this has to do with the development or modernisation of the public sector that has taken place in a number of countries in different ways over the past 20-25 years, and which in the adult education field has led to a number of economic, administrative and management-oriented reforms. The chapter discusses the general trends in this development and the consequences it has for adult education and the participants at day-to-day level.

4.1. The modernisation of the public sector

It would seem reasonable to assume that the concrete policy in the area of adult education springs from some or other combination of the official ideology in the area (dealt with in more detail in chapter 2) and the development in societal competency demands (dealt with in more detail in chapter 3).

However, it is not as simple as that. Because behind or above these approaches directly linked to adult education programmes and their functions in society are a number of more general political approaches that sketch some main lines that, among other things, have to do with the control and prioritisation of the public service functions. At the same time, policy concerning adult education is framed by some more general political considerations that not only have to do with educational policy as whole but are also to a high degree intertwined with economic policy and with labour market, social and cultural policy dimensions.

The nature and scope of the public sector is, naturally, different from one country to the other, and it is clear that the public sector has in general been larger in the Scandinavian welfare states, which form the starting point of presentation, than in most other capitalist industrial societies. But many of the features of the public sector that have been seen in Scandinavia during the last 20-25 years are also known in different varieties in, at least, most of the EU countries, North America, Australia and New Zealand. This has to do with what in Denmark has in general been termed "modernisation of the public sector".

In this connection it is also very important to be aware of the fact that this modernisation policy does not only have to do with concrete political, administrative and economic measures. At least as important are the ideological modes of perception, thinking and formulation that to a very high degree have managed to change the focus and linguistic usage concerning the function of the public sector. During the period in question, in the areas mentioned an extensive shift has taken place from an ideological and political orientation towards social welfare and efforts to ensure equality towards market-orientation and service production based on a fundamentally individualistic and competitive attitude.

This is not the place for me to go into details about the overall political change of course. I shall merely illustrate its scope and perspective by briefly listing a number of the measures for change that typically, and in various formations, form part of the more general strategy and have come to dominate the area.

Basically, it could be said that there is a transition from welfare orientation to service orientation. The function of the public sector is no longer regarded as the obligations of the community vis-à-vis its members, but more as supply of services that are to fulfil a number of the users' needs. Implicit in this is that a fundamental social orientation is being turned towards market orientation.

In extension, the implication is a belief in the orientation of the market economy in the direction of demand and supply with free competition and pricing. This involves, inter alia, the policy of tendering and privatisation that is well known in many countries. In the education area, this means that public and private suppliers can compete to supply various educational services that earlier have without question been a matter for the public sector, and that many public educational institutions can, and indirectly are forced to, find their own resources by means of 'commercial activities'.

In the wake of this, the production oriented so-called "taximeter schemes" have been introduced for the state's contribution to financing a number of educational institutions. There has been a clear trend towards an increasing share of user payment, not least in the adult education area, where the users can be individuals, enterprises and public bodies, and where in some cases short-term educated participants have been 'given sanctuary'. This is partly because previously they have not to such a great extent made use of public education and training offers, thus placing a burden on educational expenditures, and partly because it is regarded important to raise the educational level of those with brief schooling with respect to economic growth and international competitiveness, and because it is thought that they are less prepared than those with better education to pay to be educated.

"Decentralisation" has become a major code word in the area of public management. Central management has typically been changed from management by rules and regulations to "goal and framework management", and in the individual institutions responsible boards have been introduced in accordance with a management oriented concept where the customers for the education programmes' "products" usually constitute a large number of the board members, while at the same time in general efforts have been made to strengthen the power and accountability of the management. However, to an increasing extent it would seem to be clear that in practice such "decentralisation" can lead to something like the opposite. Power becomes concentrated in the central administration which lays down the frames for economy, goals and contents, after which the local implementation is left to the boards and the strong leaders whose "noses are kept to the grindstone" by means of what has become an extensive, centrally controlled evaluation practice.

With respect to personnel policy, the efforts have gone in the direction of replacing fixed rates of pay by more individual or bonus-based salaries according to functions, qualifications, responsibility and results, and at the higher levels, in particular, to replace permanent appointments by fixed-term employment.

In addition to this, on the political level, especially in recent years, there has been a clear trend towards a closed, top-down policy strategy with far-reaching orientation towards supranational bodies such as the

OECD and the EU, in contrast to earlier traditions of involving the parties concerned more actively in the decision-making processes at all levels.

The relationship of public authorities to the rank-and-file members of society has also undergone a significant change. We are no longer regarded and referred to first and foremost as citizens or fellow citizens, but as users, consumers, taxpayers, workforce, unemployed etc., to whom the public authorities relate as a kind of counterpart in an exchange of services and trade-offs. Simultaneously, the language employed concerning the activities of the public authorities has shifted from being by and large administration oriented to a more modern, smart and often almost advertising-oriented type of language.

Finally, it should not be forgotten that all this modernisation has often been accompanied by cuts. The market mechanism is being used to break down rigid bureaucratic structures with a view to making the public services more efficient. In Denmark the present prime minister is known for his political ideological manifesto entitled "From social state to minimal state" (Rasmussen 1993). It is also important to note that even though the right-of-centre parties have more eagerly pursued this new political direction, the social democratic parties have basically followed the same lines, and in the UK New Labour has even gone further than the Conservative Party in a number of areas.

4.2. Reforms and the risks on the horizon

In the field of adult education, the trends outlined above have to a high degree left their mark on the development in different countries. In the last decade, in particular, tension as been increasing between the desire to expand adult education programmes, lifelong learning and modern competence development on the one hand, and on the other hand the general policy which is to reduce state management and public expenditures. In Denmark, for instance, following extensive committee work and in agreement between the big parties, in 1999-2001 a wide-ranging reform of adult and continuing education was carried out with the aim of strengthening the area by means of strategic, administrative and management rationalisations and which also means big savings for the public sector. It was the intention that these savings should be counterbalanced by increased user payment by the participants in adult education, enterprises and local authorities. But in reality the savings have resulted in the disappearance of most of the considerable rise in participation in adult education programmes that took place up through the 1990s (Danish Ministry of Education 2002).

Falling participation in adult education could resemble a break in principle with the slogan about lifelong learning. But this is not the way it is regarded on the political level. Denmark still fully supports this slogan and is an extremely active participant in international cooperation to promote lifelong learning. This apparent contradiction does not cause any great problems, because even though the EU urges the member states to allocate increased resources to adult education (e.g. the Commission 2000), it must be said that most of the other countries that actively support the idea of lifelong learning have not followed this up to any great extent by increasing public education budgets (Field 2002, p. 28ff, Commission 2003). In the case of the USA, Sharan Merriam and Rosemary Caffarella after a thorough examination of the situation sum up as follows:

"In our society, questions of access and opportunity that trouble the adult learning enterprise reflect the disjuncture between the values we promote in our rhetoric and what actually happens. The gap between the better educated who seek out and can afford continuing learning opportunities, versus those who do not, continues to widen. Government policy and funding tend to support only efforts that directly address employment-related skills and economic return so that the United States can be competitive in a global marketplace. Large segments of the adult population do not respond to these initiatives, however. Those who do participate are already the better educated, the more socially mobile, the ones with higher income. Formal adult learning opportunities, for the most part, thus become a vehicle for solidifying a socio-economic structure contrary to our stated goals of access and equality." (Merriam & Caffarella 1999, p. 86).

At the international level, the general attitude seems to be that the obligation of the public sector in connection with investing in lifelong education is a matter of organising the structural preconditions while the costs should be borne by the users, i.e. participants, enterprises, organisations and, if necessary, the local public social authorities.

What is perhaps most worrying in connection with these trends is not so much a question of the extent of participation in adult education programmes – as will appear later in this book, under certain circumstances the participants' benefit from adult education programmes can be extremely doubtful, and it is at any rate an economic misconception to believe the value of the programmes to society and its members is directly proportional to the number of participants. To a high degree there is a qualitative and content dimension at play, and on this point there is a clear general tendency in current policy to upgrade vocational education programmes and educational elements, while more general programmes and educational elements receive lower priority. A fundamental philosophy would seem to exist to the effect that the public sector has an economic interest in supporting vocational adult education programmes, at least to the extent that users cannot otherwise be expected to participate in them, while the question of economy in more general adult education programmes is regarded as unprofitable cultural policy and in certain contexts a matter of social policy.

This is, naturally, a very convenient view when seen from a narrow economic perspective. But the question is the extent to which the argumentation is tenable. It can be seen from various OECD and EU reports that lifelong learning has to a high degree also to do with general welfare objectives including democracy and the social balance of the societies, inter alia on the basis of the conception that things are connected and that general welfare can also pay economically because it stabilises the societies, thus reducing public expenditures in a number of areas that have no direct connection with education.

Another grave problem area is the whole issue of competence. If there is any truth in the claim that adult education programmes both can and must contribute to the development of up-to-date competences in the adult population, the political trend outlined must be presumed to have a directly counter-productive effect. This is closely related to the fact that the down-grading of general education programmes and educational elements will in practice come to mean the down-grading of everything that extends beyond the development of measurable professional qualifications in the more traditional sense, and thus also reduce the possibilities of broad development of competence.

In the Danish vocationally oriented adult education programmes, the education reform referred to has led to far-reaching tightening of the financial position of the institutions, at the same time as they have forced into negotiations about regional mergers and other efficiency measures. The institutions have quite literally had to fight for survival with extensive rounds of firings etc. This means that the extensive endeavours and activities devoted to up-to-date "general qualification" or competence development in the decade between 1987 and 1997 have been completely forced into the background to the benefit of economy thinking, rationalisations and marketing.

Finally, it should be mentioned that although the aim is that increased user payment should not hit those with brief schooling, in practice the development will nevertheless inevitably lead to the enhancement of the social imbalance that is already such a prominent feature in the field of adult education. At the same time, the stepped-up individualisation also implicit in the policy pursued will generally cause problems for everyone who is not in possession of the competences necessary to manage in the changeable risk society.

Overall, this implies what the Danish education researcher Anders Siig Andersen has termed a "risk horizon" (Andersen 2002, p. 41ff), i.e. that in spite of comprehensive national and supranational efforts in research and preparatory activity, there is considerable uncertainty about what the policy will actually lead to in different areas. In my view, this is closely connected to the fact that the whole perception and thinking concerning the reform lacks a participant perspective, i.e. that there is fundamentally little interest in what all this will mean for the people whom it actually concerns, both in the preparatory activity and the reform. Therefore, I will deal with this subject briefly in the concluding section of this chapter.

4.3. The missing participant perspective

The policy in general pursued in the field of adult education is, as described above, fundamentally based on an economic rationality. This also implies that the considerations made are economic calculations.

In this way the cohesion between the objectives set up and the policy actually pursued becomes very one-sided. It is not only welfare objectives and social and cultural perspectives that disappear in the economic calculations. It is in fact also the most key societal goals that should be pursued, namely the competence development which on the level of the individual, the enterprise and nationally is claimed to be crucial for meeting the challenges of late modernity (cf. chapter 3).

When the policy pursued is compared with the reality of the many ordinary people who today comprise the majority of participants in adult education, what becomes acutely visible is the way in which neo-liberal service management thinking, the economic growth and efficiency-oriented rationales, and modern propaganda-oriented language are placed in and refer to a completely different universe than the everyday which the majority of participants in adult education fight to make cohere (cf. also quotations from Frank Coffield in section 2.4).

From the participant point of view, it is as if decision-makers have completely lost touch with the personal and interpersonal matters that comprise the everyday of the education programmes at day-to-day level (cf. Illeris 2003a, 2003f), and which form the basis of the learning and competence development that actually take place.

The largely administratively and economically justified measures have not been able to have consideration for the fact that adult education is about living people with feelings and individuality and with an identity and perception of life that have been shaken by the new knowledge and market society. After all, this is precisely why they have to receive supplementary education, have their qualifications upgraded, or be retrained. Those who just conform and adapt to different schemes and systems, but react with their own modes of perception and evasions, create for themselves niches for subjective interpretations and patterns of action that crosscut the frameworks set by the systems (cf. Leithäuser 2000), or directly offer passive or active resistance to the practical and mental structuring when they are exposed to what they experience as meaninglessness or encroachments on their everyday lives.

If the investment in lifelong learning, which has been large-scale and in many ways necessary, is to live up to the needs that the turbulent social development has created both on the social level and for a great number of people who must try to keep up with it – for otherwise they will be marginalised as societal "losers" – then economic, structural and administrative deliberations and decisions are not sufficient. Then it is also necessary to understand what happens to the people whom it concerns: what their situation and possibilities are, what they think and feel, and how it would, perhaps, be possible for them to learn something new and readjust. This does not "merely" concern acquiring a new syllabus, some new knowledge and skills, but fundamental changes in their perception of and relationship to themselves and their surroundings - readjustments in identities that have been built up over a long period and often with great difficulty.

In the next chapter, therefore, I shall discuss the issue of what important goals and modes of perception could be for an adult education policy that could be in line with the needs of both participants and society.

5. Adult education in the market society

In this final chapter of the first part of the book, the point of departure is in the participants' ambivalent relationship to adult education and from here the contours of opposition are developed that can function as a supplement to the dominant ideology and policy in the area. At the centre of this opposition is the concept of "resistancy", understood as the ability and will not merely to allow oneself to be carried along on the wave of "development", but to have an independent and critical view of the many influences we all are exposed to in late modern society. Psychologically, resistancy is a competence on a line with all the other competences that educational management is aimed at, but its special nature is that it functions as a countermeasure by questioning the uncritical practice of the other competences. On the societal level, this is about updating the human developing and liberating intentions that traditionally have been the fundamental intentions in adult education programmes. At the same time, this is necessary opposition to the inappropriate economic rationale dominating the frames and design of adult education at present.

5.1. Lifelong learning in a participant perspective

In the previous chapters I have described how the development and structure of adult education programmes have in many ways been co-determined by a number of highly different angles that society brings to bear, ranging from the ideology of lifelong learning via the development in competence demands to the current policy in the area. I have also pointed out how these factors force development forward in certain areas that are considered appropriate on the basis of political, economic and administrative premises, but which may, at the same time, be less appropriate when considered on the basis of the participants', and partly also of the teachers' and institutions' perspectives. In this chapter, I shall discuss, from this angle, on which basis the adult education programmes might be structured so that they meet the participants' needs to a higher degree, while at the same time respecting society's reasonable requirements.

Of course, there are very great differences within what might be identified as participants' needs, e.g. against the background of their generation and position in relation to the labour market (I shall return to this in chapters 8 and 9). Nonetheless, there are also some fundamental common features that apply, and they are in a way the same features which, seen from society's side, are ideologically reflected in the concept of lifelong learning. However, seen from the participants' side, the social changes that are termed late modernity, the transition to the knowledge society, the risk society, globalisation, the market society, etc., each place them in situations where adult education and lifelong learning emerge both as a necessity and a demand that impose on them relentlessly, whether they like it or not.

The day when folk high school traditions, public enlightenment, the working class movement or personal interests provided the most significant basis and momentum behind adult education programmes is vanishing. In Finland, education sociologist Ari Antikainen and others have shown how adult education for the oldest living generation was connected with managing in life, for the intermediate generation it was related to career opportunities, and for the young generation it has assumed the character of a consumer good (Antikainen 1998, Antikainen & Kauppila 2000). However, in recent years the scene has changed character yet again, and among all generations of working age there seems first and foremost to be a demand (cf. e.g. Hake 1999, Jarvis 2002). Societal development is headed in a direction where more and more people, without having desired or sought it, find themselves in a situation where learning and education appear as a direct or indirect demand and the only alternative to societal, economic and social marginalisation, or, as the situation has been described in more concrete terms by a group of education researchers in connection with a discussion on the conditions for lifelong learning already in 1996:

"Develop! Has your clock stopped? Why do you not want to learn new things? Don't you dare? Are you ready to meet the new challenges of the information society? How does your career planning look, that is after all no longer a dirty word, is it? Do you really think that you can keep your position, your job, or become anything, if you do not pull yourself together and become a bit more ambitious? Or do you perhaps want to live on handouts for the rest of your life? Show some initiative, independence. Do you want to be in on this or not? Get quality into your life. Be dressed for success, on the cutting edge. Flexible. Adaptable. Develop. Get an education!" (Nielsen et al. 1996, p. 29).

The quotation describes without restraints how the situation may feel, and in our research we saw how this applies, to a greater or lesser degree, to a very large proportion of the participants in the ordinary adult education programmes today (Illeris 2003a, 2003f). Despite all differences, there is general social pressure which, for the individual may very easily assume the character of both necessity and coercion. Seen from the bottom, the nice rhetoric on lifelong learning becomes a demand, something one must live up to, something one cannot avoid. When education becomes a demand or a necessity, something happens to the motivation and thereby also the learning. It is not at all the same as when a person tries to learn something motivated by desire or interest (I shall return to this in part 2 of the book).

Of course, necessity and interest are not inherently opposites. In most cases there is an element of both in connection with adult education, and in our research we found that precisely this ambiguity was the most pervasive feature among participants in ordinary adult education in Denmark today, which then typically causes many problems and uncertainty in the motivation and learning (Illeris 2003a, 2003f).

However, must it really be like this? Is it not possible to imagine that the considerable human and financial resources expended on adult education might be channelled in a way so as to ensure that both participants and society derive more joy and satisfaction and, at the same time, more learning, development and competence from the heaps of money and well-meaning endeavours and efforts?

The situation cannot be drawn up in such easy black and white terms. Of course, it is correct that school and education always involve an element of what the French sociologist Pierre Bourdieu has termed "symbolic violence" (Bourdieu 1998), but school and education may still also be thought of as places where a person can develop and gain richer insights, surmount barriers and limitations, add new elements to his life conditions, experience joy in life and growth, realise dreams and gain new opportunities.

These questions have for a long time had a central position for critical educationalists and educators, who have found it difficult to find solid ground for a stand against the massive tendency to consider and quantify education on the basis of (economic) efficiency and productivity. Because to all appearances education programmes have become more open to participants through e.g. more free choices, more social forms of interaction and working modes, and greater attention to the individual. However, at the same time, with the increasing economic rationale, a pressure to engage in education has emerged which, to large groups of adults, seems more relentless than ever before and which has a tendency to bury the positive opportunities which also lie in the endeavours to expand adult education and adult learning.

What may we then today set up as a beacon for developing and liberating adult education which tries not merely to conform and adapt participants to the market society subject to the ultimately always economically oriented societal conditions; adult education that endeavours to meet participants' needs and interests on their own terms and at the same time tries to contribute to breaking the unrestrained form of "development " that not only turns many people into objects for economic growth, but ultimately also threatens to decompose the very foundations of humanity? There is a need for a counter-measure, but how may it be embedded, structured and practised in a society that is clearly busy moving in an entirely different direction?

5.2. Public enlightenment, critical thinking and personal authority

If one wants to assume a stand on the question formulated above, it may be a good idea first to realise that historically there is nothing new about seeing adult education as a critical or liberating countermeasure to the dominant power relations. On the contrary, the growth of this area everywhere has been rooted in endeavours to enable adults to take charge of their own lives and in this way also further the development of society and civilisation. This applies e.g. to the development of folk high schools and public enlightenment in Denmark, to the study groups in Sweden, to British and American adult education, and to many initiatives in developing countries in the latter half of the 1900s.

It is only since the 1960s that the vocationally qualifying element of adult education programmes has emerged and gradually has pushed the more general intentions into the background. The choice need not, of course, be either/or. The two strands of intention are well able to be combined, and even be made to strengthen each other mutually. Competence development by no means excludes that personal critical and liberating development may take place at the same time, but currently all efforts relating to competence development are sweeping rapidly in the direction of increasing focus on vocationally related skills, despite all the pretty rhetoric.

However, in the tradition and history of adult education there is a solid basis for emphasising broad, general and liberating endeavours in many different ways and levels, and therefore it is also worth taking a closer look at the whole foundations upon which these currents are built.

First, it may be pointed out that there have always been two main types of argument for the broad foundations of adult education. Partly the idealistic and popular type of arguments along the lines that adults in a democratic society of course must have a decisive influence on their own education, and partly the pedagogical and learning related type of arguments to the effect that adults learn best when they are committed and have influence on what the education is concerned with and how it is practised.

The more specific development of the theories and arguments, furthermore, allows for distinction between an individual-oriented tendency in the Anglo-Saxon tradition and a more generally oriented tendency that has especially flourished in Scandinavia and Germany.

The Anglo-Saxon tradition has roots reaching back to John Dewey's and Eduard Lindeman's work in the first half of the 1900s (e.g. Dewey 1916, Anderson & Lindeman 1927) and has later been continued by, among others, Malcolm Knowles (e.g. 1973), who greatly emphasised that adult education must be self-directed, Stephen Brookfield (e.g. 1987), who especially highlighted development of critical thinking, and Jack Mezirow (e.g. 1991), who with the concept of transformative learning, with inspiration from among others Paulo Freire's *Pedagogy of the oppressed* (1970), developed a very wide horizon for adult education's boundary-breaking potential (cf. section 6.3). A shared characteristic of this American tradition is, as mentioned, the individual oriented focus on the adult's personal learning, development and control of the course.

In the North European tradition in the form that has especially developed in Germany and Scandinavia, the emphasis lies to a larger extent on more generally oriented concepts, such as "enlightenment" and not least the concept of "personal authority", which has often been posed as the target concept of liberating education thinking, like e.g. within German critical theory (the "Frankfurt School") by Theodor Adorno in a contribution entitled *Erziehung zur Mündigkeit* [Upbringing for personal authority], which was to be his last work (Adorno 1971). In this concept of personal authority, individual integrity and judgement are directly related to and placed in opposition to societal conformity and oppression, and in this way it has been able to serve as a navigation point for an understanding of adult education as a force that has right up to this day been both individually and socially rooted.

In the current situation, there may thus be ample reason to reach back to these different perceptions as a countermeasure to the conformity of adult education programmes to the short-term, one-sided economic oriented way of thinking. The concepts mentioned may play a part in maintaining that adult education may be concerned with other goals than merely vocationally focused adaptation and upgrading of skills and have another societal function as a significant contribution to the broad and socially related development and liberation of adults. However, it must not at the same time be overlooked that the mentioned concepts, both the more individually oriented from the USA and the more generally oriented from Northern Europe, today have an unmistakable aura of being related to concepts which, as an underlying motif, often have the dignified and self-reliant, bourgeois middle-class male in view, and have long since been overtaken by the efficiency-chasing, globalised and multicultural late modern society.

If the perception which these concepts express are to find any use today, they must be reformulated; they must be updated to reflect the current development in society, so as to be able to answer the concealed manipulation inherent in euphonious and seductive phrases such as "lifelong learning", "education for all" and "competence development". For such formulations are, after all, only the most obvious examples from a jungle of influences directed at us all today in an attempt to sell us a plethora of goods, concepts, perceptions and messages.

We live in a market society where nothing may be accepted at face value. Marketing is effective, professional and scientific, because it must of necessity be competitive in order to perform. It is handled with great psychological insight by advertising people and spin doctors, who merely follow the interests of the buyers, users or voters as far as profits allow, and who, of necessity, always have the interests of the stakeholders as their ultimate benchmark. This is, after all, what the market society is about.

Therefore, a countermeasure to the strong vocationally oriented tendencies in adult education besides the necessary competence goals (cf. chapter 3) must include a general orientation which is clearly understood and formulated in relation to today's market society and the way in which it functions. Up-to-date forms of autonomy, critical thinking, education or personal authority must, as a point of departure, have the character of counter-concepts that are concerned with the ability and strength to maintain one's self, one's life and world, one's own and common societal interests vis-à-vis the unrestrained and ubiquitous manipulations implemented by the blind economic forces which ultimately always direct themselves towards growth and profits.

Naturally, such counter-concepts are not to replace the official concepts such as lifelong learning and competence development. However, in the previous chapters it is, inter alia, illustrated how these very general and positive concepts may be used for covering a one-sided economic and business oriented practical policy. Therefore it is necessary also to have some concepts that are explicitly formulated as counter-concepts, so they can maintain some conceptions that may function as opposite poles to the massive tendencies to using adult education as a tool solely for development of humans as labour, without regard to what this entails in terms of human strain and costs, a factor which may tip the balance of the implications towards optimisation of the performance of the individual, which is what e.g. the focus on the concept of competence in current political thinking and politics is being used for.

5.3. Resistancy as a point of reference

An up-to-date countermeasure must thus involve a reformulation of old goal-concepts of liberating adult education, and this reformulation may very suitably take its point of departure in the very precise and forward-looking reflection which Adorno managed to include in his deliberations, i.e. that development of personal authority is ultimately concerned with development to "contradiction and opposition." (Adorno, 1971, p. 145). Personal authority is basically concerned with the courage to go against the status quo and imagine that things can be different.

It is the same thought that in critical theory has been carried on by the German psychologist and youth researcher Thomas Ziehe. In 1982, together with Herbert Stubenrauch, he published the book entitled *Plädoyer für ungewöhnliches Lernen* [Pleading for unusual learning], which through an analysis of the changed conditions attempted to zero in on new perspectives and possibilities (Ziehe & Stubenrauch 1982), and up through the 1980s, he gradually approached an identification of the essence of an alternative, e.g. with formulations like the following:

"The alternative schools will, in my opinion, not be able in the long term merely to adopt what is 'already stirring' in the surrounding sub-cultures.

Opening the school for life is only a fruitful demand subject to certain con-
ditions, because this so often quoted 'life' is by no means so innocent. [...]
The concern is ... to maintain a resistancy towards reality and not simply
opening the school to reality." (Ziehe 1984)

"I am of the opinion that school should be a contra-factual experience
space; it should, that is, attempt to offer something else than reality outside
school. [...] If school is at all able to have an emphatic (definite, ed) mean-
ing, then it must be that it completes some societal and biographical lacking
experience, that it offers some learning processes that would not have come
to be 'under their own steam'..." (Ziehe 1987)

It is true that these quotations were formulated in relation to child and
youth education, but they are at a general level and may therefore also be
used as inspiration in relation to adult education. The point is that education is to offer the opportunity for learning something other than what
one learns from everyday experience together with the qualification in the
subject or contents, that education is able to be a space where one may
put a distance between oneself and the raging seas of the market society,
see things in a larger perspective, reflect on things and through this develop "resistancy to reality".

I shall here consider this concept of *resistancy* as a point of reference
for a realistic and goal-oriented critical orientation of adult education
today. The point is first and foremost that one is able to look through reality, to look beyond the shiny surface, to unveil the unceasing flow of
manipulation, to resist and take countermeasures when one becomes the
innocent victim of the hidden consequences of the anonymous societal
"development" which the market society and globalisation lead us all
into.

This can also be formulated in more outspoken terms. For example,
Frank Coffield, the English educational researcher who was mentioned
previously, writes quite frankly and with a dash of self-irony about his
reaction to the approach of the World Bank:

"In the voluminous literature which now exists on the skills people need for

the future, one essential ingredient tends to be omitted. To put the point somewhat crudely, what we all need is the ability to detect 'bullshit' and the moral courage to expose it. Students of all ages need to develop and use a critical intelligence to enable them to challenge the pretentious promises of politicians, the patronising hype of advertisers and the flimsy claims of researchers like me." (Coffield 2003, p. 45)

Furthermore, we are not merely considering direct manipulation, but also all the indirect, unavoidable and anonymous risks and harmful impacts which we hear about almost daily in the media. The German sociologist Ulrich Beck has introduced the concept of the risk society (Beck 1992). He uses the term to refer e.g. to the fact that we can never be entirely certain of what is in the food we eat, the water we drink or the air we breathe, or that we can never know if the life situation that prevails today will do so also tomorrow. One may e.g. be unfortunate enough to have taken an education for a trade or profession that becomes obsolete, to experience that one's workplace becomes part of an acquisition, merger, rationalisation or bankruptcy, or that management gets involved in disastrous speculation on the currency markets or stock market, and behind a just slightly more distant time horizon lurk risks like climate changes and floods caused by the greenhouse effect, sterility caused by artificially developed hormone-like substances, nuclear power accidents with far-reaching catastrophic consequences, or wars and terrorism with weapons of mass destruction and ceaseless floods of refugees.

At the near level, late modern society has developed in a way so that resistancy has become an ability and attitude of decisive importance if one is to have any real control over one's life and make the ever increasing volume of daily small and great choices in a considered and realistic way. In our daily lives, we are exposed to such cascades of apparent opportunities and tempting offers that resistancy is a necessity for navigating chaos in an even slightly focused direction. We are here talking, it should be noted well, not of a resistancy that has the character of blind negativity, but is concerned with considered and balanced choices. Furthermore, in the larger context, it is concerned with combining the personal perspective with societal responsibility aiming at the sustainability that is ultimately also the foundation of the market society.

This also implies that such resistancy in members of society is not in opposition to the most fundamental premises of late modern society, but, on the contrary, is an entirely necessary prerequisite for the fundamental ideals with respect to both democracy and well-functioning market mechanisms. Whether we are considering the struggle concerning political decisions, the favour of the voters or consumers' attention and money, it is in principle assumed that ordinary people are able to make considered choices, and it is very much society's problem when election functions become opaque, consumers make irrational choices, and indifference or fleeting moods dominate the democratic processes. If the market society is to avoid undermining itself, buyers/users/voters must, through their decisions, be able to counter-balance the orientation towards increasing consumption, growth, profit and power, which necessarily form the point of departure for every salesman.

5.4. Resistancy as a counter competence

Of course the concept of resistancy is a very general point of departure for an updated critical reflection on education, but nonetheless I have found that it may be an important point of reference that may be common to the broad diversity of adult education programmes we have today. It is a point of reference which is able at one and the same time to maintain that education must contain a qualification in a given subject that is relevant in relation to the world in which we live, and at the same time must have a critical distance and constantly question reasons provided so that counter-measures may be nourished. Finally, it is a point of reference that involves making demands for active participation of students and the contribution, reflection and relating of the contents of the education to their own and society's situation and future perspectives.

Other terms than precisely resistancy could, of course, have been chosen for such a point of reference, e.g. a formulation based on "sustainability" to attach it to a concept which is an idiom relating to the global movement for responsible stewardship of the earth's resources. But resistancy has, as mentioned, the important quality that it is linguistically a counter-concept. It has also an immediately comprehensible meaning, and it is not entirely without interest that the concept has been taken from Thomas Ziehe and thereby attaches itself to a body of writings and a tradition in extension of German critical theory, which emphasises that both the objective and the subjective dimensions are covered (cf. Illeris 2002, s.126ff).

An obvious possibility might be to modernise the concept by renaming it the competence to resist. I have, however, chosen not to do so in order to avoid placing resistancy in the same line-up as all the other late modern competences mentioned in chapter 3. Placing the concept there might cause it all too easily to lose its character of being a counter-measure, something which has another intention and wishes precisely to stand up to the tendency of late modernity merely to merge everything into grandiloquent and superficial formulations. However, it is important to be aware that in actual fact resistancy *is* psychologically a competence, because relevant opposition includes necessary knowledge and insight as well as the ability and will to use this insight in relevant contexts. But in societal practice, it is another kind of competence, because it is contrary to the context which all the other competences form part of. Therefore it is important that it also has another linguistic expression, so that it does not just appear as yet another demand, but may be distinguished as something else with another intention.

At the same time, it is important that resistancy, like the other competences, is something that is broadly composed and requires a combination of many abilities or qualities. In more general terms, the American Henry Giroux thus points out in his analysis of opposition in connection with education, which provides an extension of Paulo Freire's work with the pedagogy of the oppressed (Freire 1970), resistancy is a dialectical concept in at least three different ways.

"First, it celebrates a dialectical notion of human agency that rightly portrays domination as neither a static process nor one that is ever complete. Concommitantly, the oppressed are not viewed as being simply passive in the face of domination. The notion of opposition points to the need to under-

stand more thoroughly the complex ways in which people mediate and respond to the interface between their own lived experiences and structures of domination and constraint. Central categories that emerge in the problematic of opposition are intentionality, consciousness, the meaning of common sense, and the nature and value of non-discursive behavior.

Secondly, opposition adds new theoretical depth to Foucault's (1977) notion that power works so as to be exercised on and by people within different contexts that structure interacting relations of dominance and authority. What is highlighted here is that power is never unidimensional; it is exercised not only as a mode of domination, but also as an act of opposition or even as an expression of a creative mode of cultural and social production outside the immediate force of domination. This point is important in that the behavior expressed by subordinate groups cannot be reduced to a study in domination or opposition. Clearly, in the behavior of subordinate groups there are moments of cultural and creative expression that are informed by a different logic, whether it be existential, religious, or otherwise. It is in these modes of behavior as well as in creative acts of opposition that the fleeting images of freedom are to be found.

Finally, inherent in a radical notion of opposition is an expressed hope, an element of transcendence, for radical transformation – a notion that appears to be missing from a number of radical theories of education that appear trapped in the theoretical cemetery of Orwellian pessimism."
(Giroux 2001, p. 108)

Resistancy is thus, like the competences, a concept that involves potential for action, a readiness to act and an action orientation, i.e. a certain direction in the potential actions. In extension of this, some important qualities may be pointed out which resistancy involves (and which can also be significant in connection with other competences).

Resistancy is concerned with a certain *overview* and a broad *orientation towards the surrounding world* and understanding of the overall contexts one is part of, socially, occupationally and in everyday life. I do not understand this immediately as such a subject and curriculum orientation which is typically the contents of a number of the traditional school subjects, such as history, social studies, biology, geography, religion, physics, etc., but a more overall orientation which doubtless includes elements of these subjects, but aims more towards insight into how one's world is structured and how the person him/herself is placed and may influence these contexts. In a book published in Danish (Illeris et al. 2002, cf. Illeris 2003e), I have taken part in describing how, through extensive identity processes, young people today attempt to reach a useful self-orientation that they can use for navigating the infinite options of the market society. These search processes do not cease even though the individual grows up and perhaps eventually develops a more coherent identity. On the contrary, precisely adult education shows how many attempt to use the education situation for continuing to work with such general orientation processes, and it is important that it is also part of the rationale and self-perception of adult education to give room for and further these processes.

In extension of this, one might also point to an important element of qualified *competence to choose* and *competence to act*, two types of competence which to a high degree have been part of pedagogical debate and thinking, but which are strangely absent from the lists of competences referred to in chapter 3. The debate has e.g. typically focused on young people's many choices of subject and streams within the education system, but also more broadly on late modernity's infinite number of options and the actions that flesh out the choices. As an element in the constitution of resistancy, the choosing and action competences must, however, reach further to include also taking a position on the character and reasonableness of the choice posed, to the interests that lie behind them, and on that basis the decision whether the choices are acceptable or must be rejected. This also means that one is able to act in a goal-oriented manner in extension of choices made.

Yet another important element centres on *reflection* and *reflexivity*, i.e. on being able to think through the situation and consider it in both its societal and personal contexts. Late modernity's demands in these areas have often enough been highlighted, e.g. typically and from very different angles by authors like Schön (1983), Giddens (1990) and Ziehe (1997), and they are closely related to the concept of the obligation of adult education to the development of *critical thinking* which holds a central position in Stephen Brookfield's work (e.g. Brookfield 1987). All in all, the concern is that focused control in relation to late modern society requires that the individual should be able to take a critical and considered stand, i.e. personally thought through and deliberated, vis-à-vis the countless challenges we all face constantly.

As a crosscutting element in relation to all those mentioned, I will further point out being self-contained, i.e. being self-aware both mentally and physically, strengthening one's sense of self, self-perception, insight into self, self-confidence and ultimately the identity. These matters make it possible that both competences and resistancy can be personally embedded and targeted, and thereby may be maintained as something more than scattered reactions, but as part of a pattern of life that has been personally chosen and directed.

Over against that, it must of course be part of the picture that adult education must focus its orientation on that which is shared and so ranges beyond the far-reaching individualisation tendencies of late modernity. This is i.a. embedded as a positive element in Etienne Wenger's highly current concept of "communities of practice" as the framework for adult learning processes (Wenger 1998). However, precisely as a counterweight to individualisation, I find that there is a need for a more obligating formulation than the concept of communities of practice immediately entails, something which more directly relates to the fact that resistancy does not take us very far if it is merely to be personal or individual. Therefore also *cooperation* and *collectivity* belong in the picture as key elements, in order that the resistancy may make an impact beyond the personal level.

In extension of this, I shall as a highly important element finally include the concept of *social responsibility* which is emphasised by i.a. the Belgian adult education researcher Danny Wildemeersch (Wildemeersch 1991, 1998, Jansen et al. 1998). This refers to the fact that developed competences as a counterweight to individualisation must of necessity be exercised with observance of a built-in responsibility to the totality that in the individualisation there is a tendency to atomisation, and the individual must realise his responsibility for countering such atomisation.

The concept of resistancy referred to in this book thus comprises, in interplay with the concept of competence, as significant component elements, overview and social environment orientation, competence to choose and competence to act, reflection, reflexivity and critical thinking, self-containment, and cooperation, collectivity and social responsibility. These concepts are of course in many ways overlapping, and, at the same time, many other words might be included in order to elaborate the characteristics. The words chosen are each central and necessary for providing nuances for the whole I am trying to establish, but it is only when they are combined in the concepts of competence and resistancy that they get the specific character I am concerned with here, i.e. the character of a coherent capacity for in a conscious and considered way both to work with and against the many challenges we all face, and not just unreflecting allowing oneself to be driven by the blind "development" of late modernity and the market society.

5.5. Double qualification

In the above, resistancy is presented as at once an opposite pole and a supplement to the competences which at the official level are currently described as a goal of adult education (chapter 3). It is important to establish such an opposite pole in order to stem the tendency for one-sided vocational orientation of adult education. However, it is also important to emphasise that resistancy as a goal-concept is not to replace the competence goals, but on the contrary be understood as a necessary supplement.

The competence goals and the development of the concept of competence generally invite an important renewal of thinking and practice in adult education programmes that may contribute to bringing them up-to-date with the development of society. It serves not only society's interests, but also to a high degree the participants' that such update takes place. It increases the opportunities for the participants to obtain useful benefits. They improve both the usefulness and the value of their labour and the opportunity for generally creating a satisfying life, personally, socially and financially.

With the establishment of a double aim centred on both competence

and resistancy, we thus maintain and update the strategy of double qualification which was developed in Denmark in the 1970s by progressive
educationalists and education researchers, and which i.a. formed part of
an important basis in the argumentation for the project work approach
(chapter 13, Illeris 1981).

Today, the situation is that society has completely taken over and
incorporated the approaches that were then critical and progressive and
has, at the same time, blunted them by almost imperceptibly forcing the
critical elements into the mould and premises of the dominant currents.
As may e.g. be seen in section 3.5 on the general competence demands
that have recently been formulated by the OECD, they include problem
solving, cooperation and personal attitudes and qualities. At the same
time, project work and other activity oriented work approaches have been
incorporated almost everywhere in the education systems in many countries, including especially in Norway and Denmark, and it is generally
accepted that the personal development of independence, creativity, ability to cooperate, responsibility, flexibility, etc., must go hand in hand with
the professional qualification. For the development of such abilities is
becoming increasingly necessary for late modern society to be able to
function, partly because they are important in the relentless competition
for the development of new commercial products and services, and partly because the market as the controlling mechanism in society presupposes that we all, both as workforce and through our qualified choices as
consumers, are able to contribute to the renewal processes.

Like in so many other areas, the development has caused what was
once a contribution to a critical new development so to speak becoming
adopted into society's dominant currents, and thereby at the same time
being defused of its critical potential. If the established market society
today is to have critical counterplay, as it must, because it fundamentally
places economic concerns ahead of humanity and sustainability, then it is
no longer sufficient that the members of society are qualified to think and
act in transgression of established norms. Such capacity is, of course, an
important element of resistancy, but it is not sufficient. It must also
involve that people are able, both inwardly at the personal level and out-
wardly in their activities, to say stop and to resist, to maintain themselves

mentally and to maintain common popular perspectives, to set up and maintain the demand for a sustainable situation and development, to question and in many cases even reject the options and choices people constantly face.

It is also such perspectives that I find in Ziehe's formulation on "resistancy to reality", and it can place adult education as a "counter-factual experience space", an experience space in which it is possible to question whether things might not be fundamentally different, how they might become so, and what might be done to attain this. It is e.g. absolutely necessary in the environmental and resource areas, as well as in the social, health and care areas that completely new agendas are drawn up, for these are examples of areas in which the market is well on its way towards undermining the very conditions of human existence. And the new way of thinking must come as pressure from below: in the market society it seems only to be through popular pressure and consumer choice that other control perspectives than the economic perspectives stand a chance of exercising influence.

5.6. A counterplay to economic rationality

It is also worth emphasising that the focus on both competences and resistancy can and must be seen as a counterplay to the type of economic thinking which appears to provide the foundations for adult education today.

In 2001, a book was published in Denmark with the title, *Critique of economic rationality*, (Fenger-Grøn & Kristensen 2001), formulated with a clear reference to Kant's classical work on "The critique of pure reason" (Kant 1998/1781). It contains a number of articles that disavow the economic rationality that, in the name of modernisation and efficiency, is to an increasing degree permeating the state and public functions in all areas. The tenability of this economic rationality is doubtful both on a purely economic theory basis and as viewed from ethical perspectives, and it also produces some highly questionable consequences for practical policy in a number of specific societal areas that the book addresses.

Unfortunately, the area of education is not considered in this connection, but the current trends in adult education policy, as briefly described in the previous chapter, probably provide one of the most concrete examples of how an important social and human societal concern has been treated almost entirely from an economic angle, while qualitative educational matters have played a minor role.

Such a slanting is neither appropriate nor necessary. It is not appropriate because it does not take its point of departure in, and therefore does not promote, the learning processes that are the key function of the education programmes. There is not much understanding for the fact that it concerns human interplay processes that cannot just be regulated on economic premises. It is indirectly assumed that users – the institutions, teachers and not least participants in education programmes, within the given framework – behave in an economically rational way, i.e. endeavour to optimise their benefits in the form of relevant and marketable competences. However, learning and competence development are not mechanical processes. They are highly influenced by the character of the framework conditions and the learning space in the widest sense that surround them, as well as by the participants' prior qualifications, interests, situation and future perspectives. What seems immediately economically rational may not of necessity be at the same time rational from the perspective of learning. Or, to put it in extreme terms: it is not rational to be rational if the rationality applied has not been rationally selected in relation to the reality concerned (actually, the Americans Daniel Kahneman and Vernon L. Smith received the Nobel Prize in economics in 2002 for their refutation of the assumption that humans make rational economic choices in areas of such a character).

Although this is a major expenditure area, which has a significant impact on both government budgets and international competitiveness, it is neither necessary nor appropriate to assume such economic rationality. It is not necessary because there are also other options, of which i.a. this book, a mass of concrete education practice, experiments and development work, and which most education research and pedagogical research provide examples of. Neither is it appropriate, not even on the basis of economic rationality itself, because it causes a massive "waste" in the form of insufficient learning, high dropout rates and psychological and societal problems that in combination swallow many resources, just charged to other accounts which are not considered in the economic calculations.

One can quite simply get more out of the money spent if the focus shifts to adult education that takes its point of departure in the participants' situation and interests, in participants who are not to be manipulated, but preferably qualified, and which reflects and is part of society's interests. For the time being, the control of adult education seems, however, to follow another orbit; economic rationality is obviously the prevailing mode. It must be an important part of the basis and mission of this book to paddle against this current, and instead view adult education primarily from the participants' perspective. This is also one of the reasons why the concept of resistancy has been set up as a point of reference that is to serve to maintain human and social common sense, which in my opinion is more economically appropriate for the education area in the long term than the prevailing economic rationality.

Part 2

Adult learning

The second part of the book deals with the human foundation of adult education programmes, i.e. the general and current psychological issues that impact adults' learning processes. Appropriate design, organisation and implementation of adult education programmes, apart from societal conditions, must necessarily also be based on an understanding of these psychological issues.

The starting point is a general psychological basis of perception of the way in which human learning and competence development take place. A model is set up demonstrating that all learning encompasses two simultaneous processes: an external interaction process and an internal acquisition process, and that learning always has three dimensions; the cognitive, content dimension, the psychodynamic emotional and motivational dimension; and the social and societal dimension of interaction. In addition, there is discussion of different types of learning and the question of the bodily nature of learning, tacit learning and unconscious intelligence, as well as individual and joint learning.

However, what happens when intended learning does not take place is just as important as what happens when people learn something. The next chapter deals with a number of issues and problems to do with mis-learning, defence against learning, everyday consciousness and active and passive resistance to learning.

The following chapter focuses on the special characteristics of adult learning. At the centre is the fact that adults as independent, responsible people basically themselves select and manage what they want and do not want to learn. But these choices are not always made consciously and rationally. Among other things, independence is complicated by previous experience to the effect that learning processes in schools and educational institutions are laid down and controlled by others. The chapter also takes up the questions about learning capacity in relation to age and adults' learning strategies.

But it is also clear that different groups of adults have different attitudes to learning. Just as, to an increasing extent, society places the work perspective at the centre of adult education programmes, today adults also tend to allow their learning to be guided by their work situation and perspectives, and this is part of the reason why their age greatly influences their learning interests. Matters to do with learning and ethnicity are also briefly touched on in this connection.

Part 2 concludes with a chapter on the contexts of adult learning, i.e. whether learning takes place in institutionalised training programmes, in working life or everyday life, or perhaps as virtual learning by means of modern information and communication technology.

6. Learning and competence development

This chapter is about a fundamental perception of learning. As a prerequisite for understanding adult learning within and outside of adult education programmes, it is important to be aware of what takes place from the point of view of psychology and interaction when somebody learns something. The chapter examines the processes and dimensions of learning, different types of learning and their application potential, and discusses some fundamental and general questions about learning and the body, about tacit learning and unconscious intelligence, and about individual and joint learning, including the concepts of collaborative, social, situated, collective and organised learning and the learning organisation.

6.1. The complex concept of learning

In ordinary, everyday understanding, learning means acquiring new knowledge, new skills, and perhaps new attitudes. In education programmes what is to be learned is termed subject matter or syllabus. In other places it may be something else, but the concept of learning is without meaning if there is no content: one cannot learn without learning something.

However, the modern concept of competence development (chapter 3) paves the way for a new, broader understanding of what this something can be. Competence does not consist of the learning content alone, but also encompasses the way in which one can make use of this content in known and not least unknown contexts, the way in which one relates to it, and how it plays a part in one's self-perception and possibilities for action.

With this – at last – it is beginning to be taken seriously that learning actually always is much more than content or academic acquisition. Learning also always involves something emotional and can be by marked by willingness or unwillingness and many other emotions, and they leave their stamp on what is learned. Learning is always part of some contexts, also. It takes place in an interaction between the learner and the surroundings, and the context of which learning is a part also leaves its mark on it.

In the world of reality, learning must always be understood concretely in relation to the persons and circumstances in question. Many different learning possibilities and situations exist, but a more general perception of learning can help to provide an overview and orientation in this diversity. In the following I shall outline a broader and more up-to-date concept of learning that can cover all sides of learning and thus correspond to the approach inherent in the modern concept of competence, a learning concept that I have developed and described in more detail in my book, *The three dimensions of learning* (Illeris 2002).

Here learning is, in general, understood, as all processes leading to permanent capacity change – whether physical, cognitive, skills-related, emotional, opinion-related or social in nature – and which do not exclusively have to do with biological maturation or ageing. This means that the concept of learning also covers functions such as personal development, socialisation and qualification, as the differences between these terms mainly has to do with the perspective on learning. Thus, when it comes to adult learning the whole register of mental and capacity development and readjustment processes that constantly occur are involved, and it is one of the key points of the mode of perception that it is only analytically and not in reality that one can separate the different sides and aspects of these functions.

It is, in addition, important that learning is fundamentally understood as actively constructing processes. Learners themselves develop and construct their own learning, and as a teacher, for instance, strictly speaking one cannot teach someone something but only facilitate their acquiring something. This perception of learning is called *constructivist* and was first and foremost developed by the Swiss biologist, psychologist and epistemologist, Jean Piaget (cf. e.g. Flavell 1963). In the following, while the inspiration from Piaget's own work is central, many other theoretical contributions also form part of the basis (for a more specific elaboration, reference is again made to Illeris 2002).

6.2 The processes and dimensions of learning

In order to get an overview of some of the main lines in the complicated structures of learning, I will take a starting point in an example from the everyday of adult education. This can be a teaching situation where teacher and participants discuss the rules and procedures for notice and dismissal in the Danish labour market.

The teacher is explaining the various rules, how they were formulated and the way in which one can relate to them. She/he talks and writes on the blackboard, and the participants contribute with their questions and comments. This is, thus, a *communication or interaction process* taking place between the persons involved concerning the content area that the learning is intended to deal with.

In connection with the interaction, the participants are expected to acquire this content. This can take place through an inner *mental acquisition process*, and whether or not this acquisition has taken place in the manner expected will be discovered later by the individual participants when they are in a situation where they will need it. The acquisition thus has the nature of what in psychology is called a cognitive (perception and elaboration) process. This is not only the case in education and training programmes. As mentioned, all learning processes have contents, something that is learned, and although this may not always be knowledge in the narrow sense – it can be a matter of skills, opinions, personal qualities etc. – as a rule the acquisition of content is called the cognitive side of learning.

However, not all participants learn what was intended. Some learn perhaps only some of it, others perhaps nothing at all, some misunderstand parts of it, and others learn perhaps first and foremost that they cannot understand things like rules and regulations. The absent or distorted learning may of course be due to the teacher being unable to communicate the material clearly, perhaps being more or less incomprehensible. It may also be due to the possibility that some of the participants do not possess the requisite, content-based prior qualifications on which the teacher's explanations are based. Yet a third cause may be that some are not sufficiently concentrated or committed to the learning activities. It could be that they are preoccupied with other things; perhaps they have neither the inclination nor the courage to learn anything new at the time or, more generally, perhaps they experience themselves as poorly able to understand and remember the kind of material they are supposed to; or it could be that rather more personal defence or resistance mechanisms are playing a role (cf. next chapter). In any event the learning will always bear the imprint of the character of the learner's feelings, motivation and commitment in connection with the learning process. This may be termed the *psychodynamic* side of learning, and its significance may perhaps be most clearly seen when it is reflected in the way in which the various participants relate to what they have learned.

Two participants have for instance both learned enough to be able to answer the questions that the teacher asked to check if the participants have understood the matters at hand. One of them has been strongly engaged in the review of the material and discussions, has experienced it as important and relevant, is used to considering him/herself good at handling formal matters, and will in future be able to recall and apply what he/she learned in all relevant contexts. The other may well have understood what has been said, but finds it uninteresting and irrelevant, and has only followed the programme because it was expected, is accustomed to considering her/himself poor at that sort of thing, and will in future probably not apply what she/he has learned to anything and besides forget it soon. To all appearances the two participants learned the same curriculum, but due to the differences in their motivation and feelings the value of what was learned was vastly different.

The example thus shows how the acquisition process of learning always includes two sides, i.e. a contents-oriented side, concerned with the subject matter to be learned, and an emotional and motivational side, which is concerned with the personal, more or less conscious, experience of learning and also always leaves its imprint on the result of the learning. The acquisition process has always both a cognitive and a psychodynamic dimension.

However, the example also shows that the acquisition process is integrated with an interaction process between the persons present and influenced by the situation in which the learning takes place. The interaction can take place in many different ways, ranging from pure *perception*, i.e. absorption of sense impressions, via *mediation* like in the education situation, *experience* in all imaginable contexts, or *imitation*, to the most active forms, such as *activity* and *participation*, which are characterised by the learner taking more focused part in self-chosen activities or in social context of more or less formally defined and organised character (Illeris 2002, s. 120f).

This produces a direct connection between the social context of learning and the individual's acquisition of it, and the character of this context and the degree of the learner's *involvement* and *activity* in the interaction with the environment assume considerable significance for the outcome of the learning. The environment may typically be the persons who are part of it, but it may also be influences from books, TV or other media or situations generally. In any event the environment always has a social and societal imprint, and the learning therefore also always has a social and societal dimension.

The acquisition and interaction processes of learning are closely integrated, and both types of processes must be active for learning to take place. The acquisition processes are of psychological character and follow generally a biological-structural logic, i.e. they follow the patterns that have been developed genetically over time as part of mankind's phylogenetic development. The interaction processes, on the contrary, are of social and cultural character and follow generally an historical-societal logic, i.e. they are fundamentally dependent on where and when they take place, as the opportunities for interaction are different in different societies and different historical epochs.

In addition, the acquisition processes always include two integrated sides, i.e. the *cognitive* or perception and content side and the *psychodynamic* or emotion, motivation and attitude side, respectively. The two sides of the acquisition processes gradually separate in the course of pre-school age, but are never completely separated (Furth 1987, Illeris 1995,

2002). Any cognitive learning also has a psychodynamic component, which is influenced or "occupied" by the emotional situation that surrounded the learning, e.g. whether it was characterised by pleasure or displeased reluctance, and any psychodynamic learning also contains cognitive elements: knowledge or mastery of the matters towards which the feelings are directed. The American neurophysiologist Antonio Damasio has demonstrated how the human brain functions so that the cognitive and the emotional sides always form part of an integrated interaction (Damasio 1994, 1999).

All learning thus includes two very different processes and unfolds in three dimensions that must always be taken into consideration in order to form a complete picture of a learning situation or a learning course.

The cognitive dimension develops knowledge, skills and comprehension: we strive for creating *meaning and ability* in our life so we may be able to grasp and handle it, and as we do this, we develop generally our *functionality*, i.e. our ability to function appropriately.

Through the psychodynamic dimension we strive for achieving and constantly recovering a *mental balance* or equilibrium. We use and adjust our feelings and develop through this our attitudes and motivational patterns and eventually our *sensitivity*, i.e. our ability to react emotionally, with empathy and nuances.

In the social-societal dimension, our endeavours aim at achieving belonging with or *integration in* the contexts with which we identify ourselves, and this at the same time develops our communication and cooperation potential, or, broadly formulated, our *sociality*.

These general learning conditions may be illustrated with figure 4 (next page).

Seen in relation to the current interest in competence development (as discussed in chapter 3) it is conspicuous that precisely the interconnected development of functionality, sensitivity and sociality make up the essence of the modern concept of competence. It takes this unity for the learning to take place in an appropriate way which at the same time ensures relevance and applicability in future, in the sense that the learner is able to use and develop further what has been learned, as opposed to

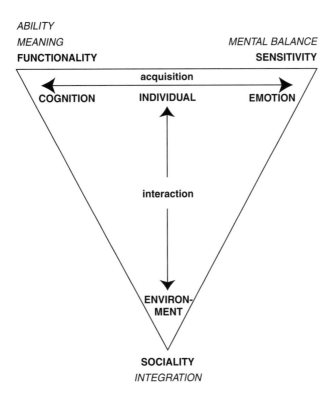

ABILITY
MEANING
FUNCTIONALITY

MENTAL BALANCE
SENSITIVITY

acquisition

COGNITION   INDIVIDUAL   EMOTION

interaction

ENVIRON-
MENT

SOCIALITY
INTEGRATION

Figure 4: The processes and dimensions of learning

e.g. the excessive emphasis on the cognitive dimension that has tradition-ally characterised the interest in learning and education.

6.3. Types of learning and application potential

One next step in the understanding of learning is concerned with the observation that the learning processes and their outcomes can be of dif-ferent character, according to the way in which the connection between the new learning and the results of prior learning is established.

The results of learning are deposited in the central nervous system as neural patterns or *dispositional representations* that may be reactivated under certain circumstances (Damasio 1994). Within psychology, resear-chers had imagined such formations, which were typically termed schemes or psychological patterns, long before the neurophysiological foundations were established. As concerns the cognitive dimension of learning, the terms used are usually *schemes* or, more generally, memory. In the psychodynamic and the social-societal dimension, we would be more likely to use terms like *patterns* or, more popularly, inclinations. Under all circumstances, it is in a constructivist understanding of learning of decisive importance that the outcome of the learning must be structured in order to be retained; for Piaget, learning was virtually identical with psychological structuring (cf. e.g. Piaget 1952, Flavell 1963, Furth 1987).

Such a structuring may be established in various ways, and based on this we may distinguish between four different types of learning that are activated in different contexts, involve learning results of different natures and are more or less psychologically energy-demanding (this is an extension of Piaget's understanding of learning, which only included what in the following discussion is referred to as assimilation and accommodation).

When a new scheme or pattern is established, it is referred to as *cumulation* or mechanical learning. This form of learning is characterised by being an isolated formation, something new that is not tied together with anything else (as described by the Danish psychologist Thomas Nissen, 1970). Cumulative learning, therefore, most frequently occurs in the first years of life, and with the passing of time only in very special situations in which the person needs to learn something which has no meaningful or personally significant context, like e.g. a telephone or PIN code number, or a list or enumeration. The learning result is characterised by a form of automation, which means that it may only be recalled and used in situations that psychologically correspond to the learning situation.

The most common form of learning by far is termed *assimilation* or additional learning, i.e. that new learning is added to an already established scheme or pattern. A typical example may be the learning of school subjects, which precisely aims to accumulate through continual addition to what has already been learned, but generally assimilative learning occurs in all contexts where one gradually expands one's capacities, whether they are of cognitive, psychodynamic or social-societal character. The learning results are characterised by being attached to the scheme or pattern in question so that they may relatively easily be recalled and used when the person is psychologically oriented towards the relevant field, e.g. a school subject, while they can be difficult to access in other contexts. Therefore there are often problems with using knowledge from a school subject in other subjects or in contexts outside school.

However, in some cases situations arise in which something happens which the person is unable to relate immediately to any existing scheme or pattern; it is perceived as something the person cannot really understand or relate to. However, if the matter seems important or interesting, if it is perceived as desirable to acquire, this may take place through *accommodation* or transgressive learning. This form of learning means that the person deconstructs (parts of) an existing scheme or pattern and transforms it so that the new elements in the situation may be attached. The person thus both abandons and reconstructs something, and it may be perceived as burdensome and energy-demanding. The person must abandon former limitations to understand or accept something that is new or different in a significant way. The result of the learning is characterised by being recallable and applicable in many different relevant contexts; it is typically experienced as having grasped something that the person has really acquired.

Finally, in special contexts a radical learning form occurs that, inter alia, has been termed *transformative* learning (Mezirow 1991). This is a form of learning which involves what one might call personality changes. It is characterised by simultaneous restructuring of multiple schemes or patterns in the cognitive, the psychodynamic and the social-societal dimension, an orientation break which typically occurs as the exit to a crisis-like situation caused by challenges perceived as imposing and unavoidable. The person has had to change in order to manage the situation and move on. Transformative learning is thus both profound and radical, it is strongly energy-absorbing, and when it succeeds, it can often also be felt directly on the body, typically as a kind of relief or release of tension.

It is important to point out here that we cannot say of any one of the four learning types that it is better than others. However, they are relevant and take place in different contexts, they are different with respect to complexity and mobilisation of psychological energy, and they are all necessary in order to arrive at the form of holistic learning which is partly inherent in the modern concept of competence, and partly optimises the development and attaining the full scope of life.

Altogether the four learning types characterise what may be at stake when a person learns something, i.e. expands his/her capacities. Together with the description of the processes and dimensions of learning in the previous sections, they make up the basis for a more complex understanding of learning which is necessary for anybody today who wants to do qualified work with specific learning processes, e.g. what characterises adult learning, because it maintains that learning may be of widely diverse character and scope, and that the entire field must always be included in the picture, that one e.g. cannot understand the cognitive subject-contents learning without also considering what takes place in the other dimensions and what learning types that are involved.

6.4. Learning and the body

When we learn something, this acquisition takes place through active chemical and electrical processes in the brain and the central nervous system, i.e. through conditions that in the final analysis are bodily anchored. Today there is much discussion of bodily learning, but how does this relate to the descriptions of the fundamental processes, dimensions and types of learning in the above? To approach this more closely, it would be appropriate to take a point of departure in some key matters concerning human development, both the phylogenetic that have to do with the development of the species through the ages, and the ontogenic, which have to do with the development of the individual.

Following this approach, one must necessarily begin with the body. In the human body, some predispositions exist from the start which are represented by the genes and formed throughout the development of the species from the monkey stage and even earlier stages. These predispositions determine both general and individual development potentialities in that they lie as unavoidable dispositions at the same time as the specific conditions for development co-determine the way in which they actually develop. If there is no damage, for example it lies in the genes that our bodies develop to a certain size, that we get arms and legs, that we develop a central nervous system that enables us to sense and process our sensation in different ways, that we can develop such emotions as anxiety, anger, pleasure and love, that we have the prerequisites to develop consciousness, speech and what we call intelligence – the so-called "higher mental functions" that the animals do not have.

Some of these predispositions develop automatically as individual development gradually progresses. The body develops by itself but is nevertheless influenced by our nutrition and other environmental conditions; for example, the absence of certain substances in our diet can result in different kinds of deformities. The higher functions are even more open to environmental influence – the language we develop depends on the linguistic influences to which we are exposed, etc. – and are therefore to a higher degree dependent on the process we call learning.

Our learning potential is thus fundamentally physically determined. Our inherited nature contains a colossal number of possibilities but some limitations also; for instance our sense of smell is not as acute as that of the dog, our sight is not as keen as the cat's, and our potential for movement is limited by body size and build. All of these potentialities are basically connected with the body's structure and functions, and in this way the higher mental functions are subject to the incredibly complex modes of functioning of the brain and the central nervous system in particular. At present, research can tell us a great deal about this but as yet does not have thorough knowledge about it.

In this context, it is first and foremost important that the human brain is a further development of the brain found in the higher mammals. The most important part of this further development consists in our high forehead, i.e. the *neocortex*, which contains the higher mental functions in particular. However, the sensory impulses we receive from our interaction with our surroundings pass from the interpretation centres for sight, hearing etc. to the neocortex, both directly and through phylogentically older parts of the brain – also possessed by the higher mammals - which are centrally situated in the brain in the limbic system, and are the seat of our emotions and a type of relay for connections to the rest of the body, including muscles, respiration, circulation etc. (Damasio 1994).

The whole of this complex mode of functioning allows us to react in two ways: emotionally immediately to impulses - we see or hear something that is perceived as threatening and react by flight or fight - and also, a fraction of a second later, we make a rational evaluation. This means that we can react immediately in an emotional way bypassing the reason, but not rationally bypassing the emotions, and that the further process, including learning that goes beyond the immediate reactions, is always regulated in an interaction between the reason and the emotions, as described in section 6.2. This applies unless the connection between the neocortex and the central part of the brain has been interrupted, either by brain damage or by a lobotomy operation – an injury that per se does not reduce reason or intelligence, but makes it "callous" in that in this way it lacks the emotional regulations that are, among other things, decisive for our interaction with others (Damasio 1994).

This all functions as a totality during early childhood development. Piaget calls the development of intelligence up to the age of two the sensory-motor period during which the child moves from simple congenital modes of reaction to more controlled and structured patterns of behaviour. It is quite remarkable that the most fundamental breakthroughs in psychology come from researchers who have worked with early childhood development: Piaget with the capacity for logical-rational thought (e.g. Flavell 1963), Vygotsky with linguistic and conceptual development (e.g. Vygotsky 1986), Freud with personality and social development (e.g. Badcock 1988) – while bodily development itself has been conceptualised by the French philosopher Merleau-Ponty (1970).

This in essence has to do with mapping the way in which the higher mental functions gradually become differentiated from the original bodily totality. The symbol functions are quite decisive in this connection, i.e. the possibility of describing and operating mentally with matters that are not directly present to the senses by means of language and signs. Normally around the beginning of school age the rational and the emotional, respectively, have been differentiated and personality formation has taken place in the sense that the child perceives itself as an independent, unique individual. About the time that puberty starts, the ability to think logically-deductively matures and a nascent identity formation has taken place in the form of a structured experience of who one is and the way in which one is perceived by others.

It is thus embedded in all of this that in a crucial way our learning is developed and co-determined on the basis of bodily conditions. However, there are some problems in our general understanding of this which in part have their roots in certain linguistic and cultural circumstances.

In the first place, what is "bodily" is in actual fact two different matters: on the one hand the learning of bodily skills that has to do with motory development and control of the body's movements and abilities, and on the other hand the emotional side of learning that is closely related to bodily expressions. This quickly becomes problematic because fundamentally learning of bodily skills is cognitive in nature. It has to do with the content of perception and learning, about learning to use one's body appropriately. It contains elements of understanding and training and it is incorporated in schemes and is developed through the types of learning already described, corresponding to and partly overlapping rational learning. One must be cautious here linguistically, because when one speaks of, for example, a skilled craftsman being able to 'feel' or 'sense' if the materials are suitable and the processing is in order, this is not feeling in the psychological sense, but precisely a matter of perception and skills, i.e. something cognitive.

On the other hand, both the bodily-skills and the rational and understanding sides of the cognitive dimension of learning as described in 6.2 always interact with the psychodynamic dimension of learning, which includes the emotions ands the mental energy associated with learning. Furthermore, our emotions are closely linked with our body, also in connection with learning. It is no coincidence that we speak of being 'pale with anger', of 'breathless excitement', of 'feeling a pang' etc. Our emotional states receive bodily expression, being reflected in the way we hold our bodies, gestures and facial expressions, respiration etc., and more or less unconsciously we teach ourselves to read others' emotions by means of their bodily expressions.

Thus, rational learning is always also tied to emotional conditions and therefore can also receive bodily expression when the emotions are bodily manifested. Similarly, bodily-skills learning is tied to emotional conditions and a double physicality can therefore be implied when learning has bodily content and the emotions linked are expressed bodily. For instance, when one learns to cycle – which is mainly bodily-skills learning although rational elements are involved too – emotional conditions can also enter in, for example, typically fear of falling and hurting oneself, and this can be bodily manifested in the form of uncontrolled movements that can complicate the learning process.

In the second place, the word "feelings" is used in two senses that are completely different in nature in this context. On the one hand, it can be a matter of feeling in the psychological sense, i.e. typically, as previously mentioned, anxiety, fear, pleasure, love and the like, that are characterised by their brain link to the limbic system and by being able to function circumventing the reason as described above. But we also speak of feeling when, for example, the craftsman feels his/her materials. This is, however, a matter of refined bodily skills that are cognitive in nature and learned by a subtle processing of many years of experience.

Finally, thirdly and perhaps most crucially, our western culture makes a quite fundamental distinction between emotions and reason, a distinction that can be traced back to the ancient Greek concepts of psyche and logos, and which not least with the cultivation of the reason during the Enlightenment and the enormous rational development of science and technology in modern industrial society has received a very central – and emotive – cultural position. We 'feel' that the great scientific and technological breakthroughs in the western world are built on our cultivation of the reason understood as logical-deductive thinking, and we thus give lower priority indirectly, and also quite specifically in our education system and thinking, to the emotions and often also the body, even though we highly value the development of subtle and humane feelings, and, for example, the bodily skills of the surgeon, the craftsman and the sportsman.

To sum up, it must be maintained here that basically all learning is bodily, i.e. tied to and developed through the potentialities and limitations of the human body, including the brain and the central nervous system. Mainly rational learning is thus also bodily related, in two ways even: in the first place in that the bodily and the rational are differentiated out from the same totality and are in constant interaction, for example, when the learning content contains elements of both and when the bodily state, for example in the form of being tired or fit set limits to rational learning. In the second place, this is the case because there is always interaction between the cognitive and the psychodynamic dimensions of learning and thus also between cognitive learning and the emotions' bodily expression.

All of this has, naturally, its concrete expressions, for example when one speaks ideologically of 'a healthy mind in a healthy body', thereby inter alia meaning that a well-functioning body is also of significance for rational learning and that therefore time must be made for breaks, sports and other possibilities for bodily activity at school. Or when one discusses the fact that the sedentary 'symbol analytical work' (Reich 1992) that many of us are engaged in can mean giving the body lower priority, which can lead to bodily diseases and can also lead to stress and the like that can result in us actually becoming worse at performing our work.

It is therefore important to emphasise that the previous sections about the processes, dimensions and types of learning cover both mainly rational and mainly emotional learning. This is precisely expressed in the process of acquisition being understood as a process that is polarised between these two dimensions that are termed the cognitive and the psychodynamic dimensions, respectively, because in the technical language of psychology these terms are more precise and thus avoid the ambiguities inherent in the more everyday concepts. In the final analysis, all the dimensions of learning have both a bodily and an intellectual side.

6.5. Tacit learning and unconscious intelligence

Another matter which may complicate the understanding of learning is the issue of consciousness. There is a mass of learning which we acquire entirely or partially subconsciously, and it has also something to do with the body, for there are frequent references to subconscious learning being "located in the body", e.g. typically when we are concerned with practical skills or emotional patterns. At the same time, in recent years there has been great interest in the concept of "tacit knowledge", which originates from the Hungarian-British philosopher Michael Polanyi (1966), and refers to the fact that humans are able to possess knowledge even though this knowledge has no nor can it be given verbal form.

The question of what it means to be conscious of something and of the relationship between the conscious and the unconscious is psychologically highly complex. Neurologically contemporary researchers like Antonio Damasio (1994, 1999) and Joseph LeDoux (2002) think that what we call consciousness consists in ongoing registering and interpreting activities in neural centres which receive signals of both outside stimuli and changes within the body. In any event, all normal humans develop an idea of what it means to be conscious of something.

However, since Freud developed the understanding of the subconscious at the end of the 1900s, it has been discussed that we also have within us something that influences us and which we are not conscious of, and that in some cases it is possible for us to become conscious of something that has thus far been unconscious.

We may thus learn something both at a conscious and a subconscious level. In both cases an acquisition takes place so what is learned achieves significance for our behaviour and understanding in the broadest sense, but only if it is conscious do we have a form of control over how we apply it. In addition a certain exchange may take place: something of the subconscious may under special circumstances become conscious, and something of the conscious may be "forgotten" or "suppressed" but nonetheless live on in the subconscious; and the subconscious learning may not merely be understood as something special or marginal. In terms of contents it may, as Freud already demonstrated be a matter of something that can exercise the highest degree of determining influence on our lives and behaviour, and in terms of volume, "occupy" the subconscious at least as much as the consciousness. The Danish psychologist and psychotherapist Ole Vedfelt writes:

> "Every moment we receive ... an incredible volume of unconscious information that influences our lives in countless ways. We can read faces and body language while simultaneously registering our own emotions, evaluating them and relating them to the general norms for emotions and behaviour. They organise themselves in emotional and social skills and in forms

of judgement of character that permeate our everyday lives as an invisible but absolutely indispensable nutritive salt. These skills do not seem to build on linear, rational thinking based on logical conclusions. On the contrary, it would appear that we take in countless impressions simultaneously, integrate them into wholes and patterns, and compare them with our prior experience taken from a formidable fund of practical knowledge. But we are not fully aware of it when we make use of this knowledge, and we do not remember where it originated." (Vedfelt 2002, p. 51)

One of the most elusive aspects of studying learning is the relationship between the conscious and the subconscious. Not only do the two levels interact, but the transition is blurred. We have e.g. a concept like "hunches" to express this experience, and the two levels may very well be in mutual conflict: we may e.g. have a conscious opinion on something and at the same time experience feelings that resist, take a different direction or make blockings.

Again, learning to ride a bicycle can be a good example to capture the complexity. While we learn it, we exert a high degree of conscious effort. We are almost excessively attentive to everything that is going on, and we make the greatest effort. However, it is not only cognitive skills learning. There are certainly also a large amount of feelings involved, and the fear of falling is, at a subconscious level, a determining factor in our behaviour, often in an inappropriate way. Once we have acquired the skill, the exercise of it is entirely "mechanical", i.e. subconscious, we "do not think about it", in fact we are quite well able to think of all sort of other things while we are riding the bicycle, and in fact balance only becomes a problem if we begin being conscious of it and try to correct the automated patterns of movement that are now "embedded in the subconscious".

Learning thus contains a complicated interaction between consciousness and the subconscious; they cannot be separated and each has its own indispensable mission. In my model for learning processes and dimensions I have therefore not included this dialectic, but the two levels are, like the bodily and the intellectual sides, present and interact across the entire field. It is, however, important to realise that even though education, as opposed to therapy, is normally only operated at the conscious

level, the subconscious level is also always active. It can be both a prota-
gonist and an antagonist, and in connection with learning processes that
are rejected or distorted, the subconscious often plays a highly significant
role, indeed. I shall return to this in my next chapter.

6.6. Individual and joint learning

In the above, learning was first and foremost considered as an individual
process. It does include the individual's interaction with his/her environment, but the acquisition process is an individual matter, and so is the
learning outcome. The social dimension of learning is irrefutable. However, it cannot stand alone.

The fact that the inner psychological side of learning is individual
does not, however, exclude that human may be learning something
together. We have all tried this, and there may be varying degrees of community surrounding learning, like e.g. a joint project in which everybody
has the same goal, group work in which the participants share the contents and research a theme or an issue together, or a more random social
situation, a discussion or a conversation.

A focused effort to learn something together may be termed *collaborative* (i.e. co-operating) learning. This concept was developed in the course
of the 1990s in connection with learning via modern computer programmes: "computer-aided collaborative learning" (CSCL – cf. e.g. Dillenbourg 1999), and in Denmark Lone Dirckinck-Holmfeld demonstrated already in 1990 that there is a great difference between learning
processes according to the character of cooperation. When participants
are together working on a joint project, there may be what she calls "genuine collaboration", i.e. cooperation in which individuals in effect joint a
fellowship of learning and developing something together (Dirckinck-
Holmfeld 1990).

However, the term "collaborative learning" may also be appropriate in
other contexts because it refers precisely to the fact that learning is
acquired individually but that individuals work together on this, and
thereby achieve a number of advantages, like e.g. that there are more
impulses, opportunity for immediate feedback and for developing under-

standing in community. This means that the social dimension of learning has a special character, and that the interaction of individuals with the environment is co-ordinated in a community. However, it does not in principle change the learning processes and dimensions as they have been described above.

The concept of "social learning" is also sometimes used in this sense, but this is less appropriate, first and foremost because it is also used in other and very different contexts and thereby assumes rather floating and imprecise status. This is because different theoreticians of learning have highly diverse perceptions of the place of social elements in learning (cf. Rogers 2002) – ranging from the one extreme that learning is "inherently" something individual which may then possibly be used for something social, e.g. when a person is to learn to behave "properly", i.e. in accordance with current social norms, to the opposite extreme that learning is in its very essence something social that develops in community and subsequently is deposited in the individual, as it is viewed most radically through the optics of social-constructionists (e.g. Gergen 1994). A third position, which in recent years has found wide acceptance, is that of Etienne Wenger, who develops what he calls "a social theory of learning" in his book on communities of practice, i.e. a theory that places the social element as the basis for the understanding of learning, but which at the same time acknowledges that there is an individual element (Wenger 1998).

In the above I have correspondingly maintained that there is both a social and an individual element in learning, but as equal dimensions inherent in all learning. Hence, I prefer avoiding the term "social learning" because all learning is at once both individual and social, and it is therefore only possible to talk of the social side or dimension of learning if the terminology is to possess an adequate degree of precision.

Also the concept of "situated learning" has, in recent years, gained widespread currency, especially after Jean Lave & Etienne Wenger published a book on the topic (Lave & Wenger 1991 – cf. section 10.1). Strictly speaking, it refers to the fact that all learning is influenced by the situation or context it forms part of, but there is, not least with Lave and Wenger, a tendency to use the concept more specifically about learning that takes place in everyday life and working life as opposed to the institutionalised or "scholastic" learning in schools and educational institutions (Wackerhausen 1997). In any event, the term refers to the interaction between the learner and his/her environment, and thereby also first and foremost to the social and societal dimension of learning.

The concept of "collective learning" is often used in the same sense as collaborative learning. However, this use of language is misleading, for if learning itself is designated as collective, it must imply that everybody learns the same. As the acquisition process, however, is individual and involves the individual prior qualifications and presumptions, collective learning proper can only take place when participants possess uniform prior qualifications both in terms of knowledge and emotions in a given area, and receive uniform input. In today's individualised society this is very rarely the case. It occurs typically in emotionally charged situations of a religious, political or similar nature, in which common feelings, common convictions or a common struggle is the central element. Many in the individualised society may have an unfulfilled need for such absorbing fellowships and try e.g. to find what they are looking for in large-scale sporting and musical events, or in sects or similar movements.

Finally, I must mention in this connection the concepts of "organisational learning" and "the learning organisation", which are today widely applied within organisational and management psychology (e.g. Argyris & Schön 1996, Senge 1990). In some cases, the terms merely refer to the individual learning by employees in an organisation or in a workplace, in which case the term "organisational" refers to a specific situation which, like all other situations, influence learning, and that this learning may be developed in collaboration. However, often the concepts represent the idea that an organisation is able in itself to learn something. With the concept of learning that has been described above, it must, however, be maintained that learning is tied to the employees of the organisation; an organisation may store the results of learning in its documents, computers, procedures, modes of cooperation, etc., but even the most advanced organisation cannot learn something in the complicated and sensitive sense inherent in human learning.

7. Mislearning, defence and resistance

While the previous chapter dealt with what happens when one learns some-thing, this chapter takes up the issue of what takes place when one does not learn something one could have learned or which one was intended to learn. Among other things, because to an increasing degree adult education has become something that the participants have entered into more or less against their will, the problems to do with different types of non-learning have also become more common. In this chapter a distinction is made between mislearn-ing, different types of mental defence, not least everyday consciousness and identity defence, and active and passive resistance to learning. All of these forms are present today in most adult education programmes. They cannot be avoid-ed and can be difficult to deal with, but in spite of this they can be simpler if one has an understanding of what is going on.

7.1. When learning fails

The previous chapter dealt with what happens when one learns some-thing. However, it is equally important, not least in connection with edu-cation, to look at what happens in all the situations where one could learn something but does not, or perhaps learns something completely other that what was intended.

It actually happens very often, perhaps more often than the opposite, that possible or intended learning is not realised. When for example, one watches the news on TV, as a rule one retains very little of it, and corre-spondingly in many other daily situations. We only pay attention to some-thing of significance to us, i.e. we select on the basis of our own criteria what means something to us personally. Furthermore, what we remem-ber or learn in no way has to be "correct" or "objective". Very frequent-ly we acquire the influences we receive in a form that fits in with our own presumptions and interests, and others who receive the same influences get something else out of them.

These matters are widespread in formalised education also. If everybody learned what was intended, then, for example, we would have no need to give grades because then everyone would only have to be awarded the highest grades in everything. In addition, one sometimes also here learns something quite different from what was intended. For many people, the most significant benefit from nine years of teaching in arithmetic and mathematics can be: "I don't understand maths", just to take one single, well-known and actually rather dramatic example.

Traditional learning psychology has not dealt with these matters to any great extent. But they have partly been studied in other contexts where, as a rule, the approach has not been one of learning theory, but has, for example, had to do with forgetting, mental deviations, brain damage, or societal perspectives such as the sorting function of the school, social heritage etc.

In the following, by relating to the learning-theory considerations in the above and to contributions from other disciplines, I shall try to achieve some clearer categories and perceptions in this important area.

7.2. Non-learning

One of the few learning theorists who have dealt more closely with these matters is the British educator, Peter Jarvis (Jarvis 1992, Jarvis et al. 1998). He uses the concept of non-learning for all situations where possible learning does not take place, and defines three categories of this: *presumption* implies that one already has an understanding of something and therefore does not notice new learning possibilities; *non-consideration* implies that while one may register new possibilities, one does not relate to them, for example because one is too busy or may be unsure about what they can lead to; *rejection* means that one more consciously does not want to learn anything new in a certain context.

Jarvis' categories thus cover three degrees or levels of consciousness in connection with non-learning, but it can be difficult to distinguish between them because they are defined by means of brief, general descriptions without any clear criteria. However, it is clear that in a very large number of cases, we simply do not relate to possible learning, that we let something go in the one ear and out the other, and that this most often takes place more or less unconsciously or automatically.

To achieve a more specific understanding of why this is the case, it is, however, necessary to dig more deeply into how learning takes place and why. A distinction must also be made between when nothing at all happens, so that it really is a case of non-learning, and when some trace is nevertheless left which also is a kind of learning, just not the learning that was intended or which the situation offered, perhaps learning in a completely different dimension – for example, a small contribution to the above-mentioned learning: "I don't understand maths" – or perhaps a simple misunderstanding or mislearning.

"Pure" non-learning may not be as widespread as one would think. On the basis of Jarvis' categories, it could be that in the area of "presumption" a strengthening or nuancing of the existing presumption takes place, that in connection with non-consideration a trace is left of the fact that one has bypassed something, or that when a more conscious rejection takes place that which lies at the basis of the rejection is cemented. Such traces are also a form of learning that perhaps when repeated can gradually be strengthened and built up into something important and meaningful – as precisely in the mathematics example above.

There are thus innumerably many degrees and nuances in this field, and when one learns something and when one does not may not be so haphazard at all. In the following I shall try to examine more closely some important areas where it is not just a matter of non-learning, but that learning in some way or other does not just take place in an uncomplicated and direct manner.

7.3. Mislearning

In a great number of cases where possible or intended learning does not take place, it is a case of simple *mislearning*, i.e. that in some way or other what happens is what we in ordinary everyday language would call a misunderstanding or failure of concentration occurs, so that the individual does not really understand or catch what is going on, or, in an educational situation, what should be learned. From the point of view of learning, it is most frequently a matter of an assimilation that is characterised by the fact that what is assimilated is in one way or other incorrect.

Everybody has the results of such mislearning embedded in their "knowledge", "perception", or "memory", and as long as this has no serious consequences, it does not matter very much. I have found an everyday example in the work of the American psychologist, Robert F. Mager, who has worked with programmed learning. He was to develop a programmed course in elementary electronics, and during prior testing of the students he found out that even though they all claimed that they did not know anything about electronics, nonetheless they all had a great deal of knowledge and understanding of the area, some of which was misknowledge and misperceptions (Mager 1961). All of them, without it being a matter of education or training, had still learned something about electronics. Although some of what they had learned was wrong, it was only when they were to apply it in a more goal-directed context that they discovered this, and then the mistakes were, of course, corrected. One can thus very well live with one's mislearning, but if it has serious consequences in a new context, one does something about it. From the point of view of learning, this can take place through an accommodation, and this is where one typically gets an "A-ha! ..." experience: "A-ha, that's the way it works!"

But it can also be the case that mislearning is built on, and as learning takes place through a combination of the new and what has already been learned, more extensive misperceptions can thus develop. For example, it could be imagined that one had gathered the impression that $2 + 2 = 5$, and if one were to further develop one's arithmetical skills on this basis, something would have to go wrong at one point or another. But as it would then be discovered and corrected, this type of mislearning does not normally have any great consequences.

In many other cases, however, what is right and what is wrong is not always so obvious. For instance, a teacher may have a quite decided and well-founded perception of how a fairy tale should be interpreted, but if one of the participants experiences it in a different way, it cannot simply be said that this is a case of mislearning. In fact, something similar probably also applies to most everyday matters and to everything that has to do with emotions and interpersonal relations. It can be difficult to draw the borderline between what can be termed mislearning and what is rather disagreement. At one time it was definitely a case of mislearning if one believed that the world was round.

In an educational perspective, mislearning is thus easiest to understand in relation to content areas where right and wrong can be clearly established. Clearly established mislearning can be corrected relatively easily – that is, if it is discovered. Mislearning must, naturally, be avoided as far as possible in education programmes, but a clear distinction between mistakes and non-mistakes can only be drawn in limited areas. If the participants always get to know what is right and what is wrong, what one may do and what one may not do, etc., they do not develop their judgement, independence and responsibility, – and in a way this is a type of mislearning, or at any rate contrary to the official objective of the education programmes.

In areas where there can be no doubt that mistakes have been made, an effort must naturally be made to avoid them and to correct them when they nevertheless occur. But, apart from this, it is quite important to hold on to the fact that *different* learnings always take place, because, as emphasised earlier, learning is always a matter of something new being linked to what is there in advance, and what is there in advance is always different. Sensitivity, dialogue and tolerance are necessary. Both for the individual and in general terms, progress may be something that takes place when something is understood in a different way than it usually is.

7.4. Defence and everyday consciousness

In many cases – probably mostly where adults are concerned – when non-learning and mislearning occur, the background is one form or another of *mental defence*. We do not learn what we can or what we should because, more or less consciously, we do not want to or cannot manage to learn it.

The concept of mental defence mechanisms is closely linked to Freud and appeared very early on as a key concept in the development of psychoanalytical theory. The classic example is "repression" as a defence against unacceptable instinctive impulses, mental conflicts and acknowl-edgement of traumatic experiences, but by degrees Freud also referred to many other defence mechanisms, and in the classic book on the area his daughter, Anna Freud, lists a great number of different types of defence mechanisms (Freud 1942).

Such defence mechanisms are, naturally, also active to a high degree in learning contexts, and can lead to blocks against learning and distor-tion of what is learned. However, the classic defence mechanisms are only of limited interest for a general perception of learning because they are closely linked to the personality of the individual. But in late modern society a type of general defence mechanism has developed which we all share and which is directed precisely at our learning.

The background to this is that all adults in our complex modern socie-ty are constantly exposed to such an overwhelming volume of informa-tion and impacts that psychologically it is impossible to absorb it all. Sort-ing must take place and this happens by us building up a defence that we insert between the influences and our acquisition of them, i.e. between influences and learning: we do not immediately learn the content of the influences. We are forced to defend ourselves against both the number of the impacts and often against their nature also. Just think of all the terri-ble events with which we are presented in a TV news programme that lasts for 30 minutes. If we were to relate in an open and receptive way to it all, the result would quickly be a mental breakdown.

This is why people in modern society develop not only personal de-fence mechanisms that are triggered in certain contexts, as Freud de-scribes the concept. We also have to develop a larger, coherent defence system, or what the German social psychologist, Thomas Leithäuser, has termed an *everyday consciousness* (Leithäuser 1976, 1992, cf. Illeris 2002, 2003d, 2004).

Everyday consciousness works in the way that we develop some so-called "theme-horizon-schemes", i.e. that within a certain subjectively defined theme or field of perception we adopt a certain impression or mode of perceiving the way things function and are connected. When we then encounter an influence which we attribute to the theme in question, in principle we can deal with it in one of three ways. We can completely reject it, i.e. avoid any kind of acquisition – which can possibly have other consequences for learning as outlined above. There can be a mental distortion so that we perceive the influence in accordance with our theme-horizon – i.e. a "distorted assimilation". Or we can "let it go straight in", thereby accomodatively altering the scheme in question in accordance with the new influence. The latter requires, as a rule, "thematisation", i.e. more goal-directed processing, because special mental effort is required to transgress and reconstruct the schemes that were developed.

In this way everyday consciousness functions both as a necessary defence and as a kind of broad and general form of what we in more acute forms term prejudices. In this way, too, adults' learning potential is less flexible than that of children and young people: the more cemented the theme-horizon-schemes are, the more frequently we have utilised them and thus reinforced them, the more difficult they are to transgress. With another expression from another psychological tradition one can also say that with everyday consciousness we can avoid the experience of "cognitive dissonance" (Festinger 1957), i.e. of contradictory perceptions.

Within adult education the question of everyday consciousness is quite central in that if the participants are to learn anything other than knowledge and skills that are in extension of what they already know and can do, as a rule a thematisation or transgression is necessary. This is intellectually and emotionally demanding and therefore presupposes both strong motivation and a situation or context that contains such a degree of social security that one dares to "lower one's defences". It is obvious that the school culture in general, the form of teaching and not least the teacher as a person are of great importance in this connection.

7.5. Identity defence

Identity defence is another type of defence that has been more generally developed in late modern society. As a general psychological phenomenon, the development of personal identity is linked to the individualisation that in earlier centuries, accompanied the transition from the old feudal society to the more modern industrialised and capitalist society. It has to do with experiencing oneself as a unique individual and the experience of how one is experienced by others. Identity is typically formed in the years of youth, and the "classic" perception of the concept was developed by the American psychologist and psychoanalyst, Erik H. Erikson, in connection with his analysis of the psychology of the phases of youth (Erikson 1968). However, it is a characteristic of late modernity that identity development to a lesser extent finishes with a fixed identity formation. The consciousness of the swift pace of change in late modernity and the demand for readiness for change bring with them tendencies for the development of so-called "multiple" identities, or perhaps rather the creation of a limited "core identity", supplemented by a layer of flexibility (cf. Illeris 2003e).

However, it is still characteristic of most adults in our society that their "adulthood" psychologically is precisely linked to a fixed and stable identity embedded in vocation and education, in familial relations and, perhaps, also in e.g. political or religious convictions. Such an identity, developed in the course of many years, usually implies that an identity defence has also been established, i.e. that one has developed mental barriers that can catch influences that could threaten the established identity. Such identity defence precisely finds expression in adults in learning and educational situations aimed at change, retraining or personal development.

For example, if for 10-15 years or more one has had a certain job and has experienced oneself as well-functioning and well-qualified in that context, and one suddenly finds that one is unemployed – not because one is not good enough, but because the company is cutting down, production is moved to another country, or the work is automatised – then one enters a situation where, against one's will, one must break down the existing identity and build up a new one, i.e. one is faced with a demand for a transformative learning process.

This is the background today, in many different forms, of a great number of the participants in adult education, and to the extent that they do not fully acknowledge and accept the situation, it will be a case of identity defence which not infrequently – and for the slightly older and in particular male participants – can prove an enormous obstacle to the intended learning processes.

But it is also the case, to a less pronounced degree, for many other participants in adult education who have not completely accepted that the education in which they find themselves is appropriate or necessary for them.

7.6. Active and passive resistance

Although it is not always so easy to distinguish in practice, there is a fundamental difference between mental defence and *mental resistance*. While defence is something that is built up or developed and lies ready to deal with certain types of influence, resistance is something with which one reacts when one encounters influences or situations that seem objectionable or threatening or which in some other way are so unacceptable that one neither can nor is willing to put up with them. One could also say that while defence is typically aimed at the mental acquisition processes of learning, resistance is to a higher degree aimed at the social and societal interaction process of learning.

For this reason, defence is also something that generally gets in the way of relevant learning, while to a high degree resistance in itself can imply or promote learning, and can even be the motive force in extremely far-reaching and transgressing learning processes (cf. Illeris 2002). In some cases there may be both defence and resistance at the same time that can make the situation more complicated, not least for the learner.

Active resistance to learning as a mental way of functioning is usually already established in early childhood in situations where one of necessity must learn to limit and control one's behaviour and activities, but it probably is most markedly something that belongs to the period of youth and can typically play a very important role in the identity formation described in the above. By means of resistance, for example, decisive development and acknowledgement of one's own viewpoints, possibilities and limitations can take place.

In adult education, active resistance is probably less frequent, but on the other hand it is typically less tentative and clearer, sometimes almost unshakeable, in form. Maybe precisely through some challenging learning processes during the years of youth, the adult has landed on some viewpoints, convictions and patterns of reaction that form elements of a more consistent identity. The borderline between resistance and defence can, in this way, become even subtler, but in general the starting point of resistance is more conscious and deliberate in nature, while to a greater extent defence functions on the automatic pilot. Therefore, in principle new learning can also indirectly form part of resistance while defence must be broken down or transgressed if significant new learning is to take place.

On the other hand, *passive resistance* is more widespread in adult education and can be expressed in very many different ways that can be irritating and inappropriate in a learning context. The Danish psychologists, Peter Berliner and Jens Berthelsen, have termed the phenomenon, *passive aggression*, and have pointed out that it contains "a protest and an energy to want something else" (Berliner & Berthelsen 1989) – which again is different from defence which precisely does not want anything else. But in some cases active resistance is withheld. The challenge is not found sufficiently important to throw oneself into active protest. Perhaps one feels disempowered in advance, which causes the resistance to find expression in various indirect ways. The consistent reaction is, naturally, that one stops and drops out of the education programme. But in many cases this will lead to some totally unacceptable and insurmountable consequences and then instead one simply mentally steps back and becomes indifferent. Nonetheless one can often not resist making irritated and irritating remarks or in other ways creating a disturbance, more or less demonstratively.

It is important here to maintain that passive resistance actually also contains an important learning potential, and that it can help to resolve the situation and contribute to important learning processes if the resistance can be brought out into the open. On the other hand this often presupposes that the teachers or other participants can see through and identify the situation as a type of passive resistance, and have the courage and the energy to take a possible confrontation.

8. Adult learning

This chapter focuses on what is special about adult learning. Firstly the question is taken up as a difference between the way in which children and adults typically learn, and it is clarified that the difference has mainly to do with how the learning is managed, i.e. the way in which what is learned and what is not learned is decided. In addition, a difference in capacity exists related to adults' possibility of thinking in a logical-deductive manner and their need for a cohesive understanding. Then questions to do with the speed and quality of adult learning are discussed, and finally the special strategies that adults typically practise in connection with a course of learning they have not chosen on the basis of desire and interest are dealt with.

8.1. Learning and life phases

The concept of lifelong learning basically contains the simple message that learning can and should be something that takes place throughout life. This premise raises the key question of whether learning processes are identical and progress in a similar manner throughout all life phases, or if there are essential differences.

For the traditional psychology of learning, there are no age-conditioned differences. Learning has been studied as a common phenomenon, for which researchers endeavoured to discover the decisive and basic learning mechanisms, and research and tests often observed animals and humans in constructed laboratory situations.

Also in relation to adult education, many scholars and researchers have claimed that adults' learning as a psychological function is basically similar to children's learning. This was, for instance, the underlying assumption behind the massive resistance to the American educator Malcolm Knowles' launching of a separate discipline of "andragogy", dealing with adult education and learning and at the same time limiting "pedagogy" to the area of children's' upbringing and schooling (e.g. Knowles

1970, Knowles et al. 1984, Hartree 1984, Davonport 1993). More recently, the British educator, Alan Rogers, in connection with his very fine description of adults' learning, has deliberately maintained "that there is nothing distinctive about the kind of learning undertaken by adults" (Rogers 2003, p. 7, cf. also Rogers & Illeris 2003).

However, the perception of learning described in the previous chapters clearly involves a different interpretation. When learning includes, among other things, the interaction between the individual and his/her environment, age-determined differences must of necessity occur because this interaction is essentially different during different phases in the course of a life. But there are also differences in the cognitive and the psychodynamic dimensions.

The special character of adult learning is most clearly seen by placing adult learning in relation to learning during childhood. In general terms, a child's learning may be characterised as a sort of conquest. The child is born into an unknown world, and learning consists in acquiring as much as possible of this world and learning to handle it, in parallel with the process of progressive biological maturity that makes this acquisition possible. However, this is seen most clearly during the first years of life when it is possible almost day by day to observe how the child, with boundless energy acquires its environment physically, socially and mentally, e.g. how the child step by step learns to communicate, to control its movements, to distinguish between a number of persons, functions and situations, etc.

Viewed in relation to subsequent life phases, there are two features of the learning process that figure especially prominently in the young child. First, that the learning is comprehensive and uncensored: the child acquires everything it can, plunges into everything, subject only to the limits imposed by its biological development and the character of its environment. Second, that the child implicitly trusts the immediately accessible adults. It is, so to speak, limited to their help and to their views and attitudes, and the child has fundamentally no possibility for assessing or choosing what the adults present to it. It must, for instance, learn the language and the dialect they speak, the culture they are part of, etc.

This is fundamentally the state that prevails throughout childhood until puberty. The child's conquest of its world is, in principle uncensored and trusting, its endeavours unlimited and indiscriminate, and it avails itself of the opportunities that offer themselves. However, this is only in principle, because in today's complicated world, the child is unavoidably faced with a multitude of mediated or secondary opportunities for experience or patterns of significance in addition to its immediate environment, not least from the mass media, but also from e.g. comrades' preoccupation with and mediation of the chaotic world of adults. The overwhelming volume of opportunities for secondary experience complicates the situation significantly and today has a major impact on the later part of childhood. It renders learning far less secure, contradictory, and less manageable, and it may provoke defence, selection patterns and mistrust, and thereby also disturb the image of the uncensored and trusting approach, which must, however, be maintained as the point of departure and basis for learning in childhood.

Opposite this stands learning during adulthood. Being an adult essentially means that an individual is able and willing to assume responsibility for his/her own life and actions. Formally, our society ascribes such "adulthood" to individuals when they attain the age of 18. In reality, it is a gradual process that takes place throughout the period of youth, which, as we see it today, may last well into the 20s or be entirely incomplete if the formation of a relatively stable identity is chosen as the criterion for its completion at the mental level (which is the classical description of this transition provided by the American psychologist Erik Erikson, cf. section 7.5).

As concerns learning, being an adult also means, in principle, that the individual accepts responsibility for his/her own learning, i.e. more or less consciously sorts information and decides what she/he wants and does not want to learn. The situation in today's complicated modern society is after all, as described in the previous chapter, that the volume of what may be learned far exceeds the ability of any single individual, and this is true not only concerning content in a narrow sense, but also applies to the views and attitudes, perceptions, communications options, behavioural patterns, lifestyle, etc. that may be chosen So a sorting of input must of necessity be made.

Swiss adult education researcher Pierre Dominicé thus writes, on the basis of a number of biographical studies:

"Their struggle for the independence to become themselves is a central factor in adults' interpretation of their life histories. 'Being adult means to be autonomous', writes one participant, who adds, 'There is not a right age to reach this autonomy of adulthood. It depends so much on factors such as family, school, and life and how we find peace within these dimensions'." (Dominicé 2000, p. 65)

8.2 Responsibility for own learning

The most fundamental difference between children's learning and adults' learning is thus related to how the learning is controlled. In recent years, this matter has, however, been much debated from a somewhat different angle, i.e. the debate on "responsibility for own learning". In Scandinavia, this debate has especially been directed at youth education programmes, the background for this being that young people have not been as willing to learn "what they have to learn" as was previously the case if they have not been able to see or accept the intention behind it. In so doing, the young people *have* actually, in their own way, to an increasing extent assumed responsibility for their own learning, or, at any rate, their own non-learning. The underlying opinion of many debaters has, however, been that young people should themselves assume responsibility for learning what somebody else has decided.

For adults, the problem is somewhat different. As a point of departure, adults clearly want to decide what they want to learn and do not want to learn. The very nature of adulthood involves both legally and psychologically that one assumes responsibility for oneself, one's actions and opinions. This is the general situation of learning in everyday life, and thus adult learning is by nature self-directed – and, strictly speaking, the issue of self-direction as discussed by Malcolm Knowles (1973, 1975) and many others can never be a discussion about learning but only about education and organisation (cf. the concept of participant direction as introduced in section 12.1).

But when adults then enter into institutionalised learning situations, a kind of regression often takes place: they easily slip back into the pattern they know so well from their schooldays. They leave responsibility in the hands of the teacher, and the teacher is also almost always willing to assume responsibility, and even parts with it only reluctantly (cf. Illeris 1998). In this way, there is a reversion to childhood, leading to a highly ambivalent situation in which the adult participants both want to and do not want to decide for themselves.

Most adults, except perhaps the youngest, appear somehow to have acquired the perception that institutionalised learning is something that belongs to childhood and youth. When, as adults, people participate in courses and training programmes, they typically use the phrase "going back to school", and this phrase typically reflects the feeling of reversion to childhood, disempowerment and perhaps even humiliation that lies just below the surface of many people who have not made a clear individual choice to be in the learning situation.

As the Australian educator, David Boud, has documented (Boud 2003), adults in general do not like to be labelled as learners, not to say pupils. Because then it is precisely the case that others decide what the individual is to do, that the individual is stripped of the authority of an adult, and that the individual is not good enough as he or she is, because then obviously the whole thing would not have been necessary. This sentiment has deep roots, it necessarily has an impact on the learning, and teachers often tend to suppress the fact that it is so. Therefore we often hear in adult education programmes the phrase: "We *are* adults, aren't we?", spoken as a sort of mantra in situations where the similarity with the submission of childhood learning becomes a little too insistent.

There is, however, no doubt that the learning progresses best when adults themselves accept decisive responsibility. But this presupposes that the framework of the education programme provides opportunities for such responsibility, i.e. that not too much has been decided and determined in advance, that the teacher consciously provides space for it, and that the content of the programme makes it fundamentally possible for adult participants to learn something which they themselves think is important and meaningful.

Thus, the question of whether the intended learning is or may be subjectively meaningful becomes entirely decisive for adult education programmes, and the answer lies in the participants' situation in life, their backgrounds and their interests. From the point of view of learning, "adulthood" is typically dominated by having some strategic life projects that spawn a multitude of things to do and attitudes that fill up the individual's life, and at the same time provide the benchmark for what one learns and does not learn. Some cases involve clear and conscious choices, but very often decisions are made more or less by the "automatic pilot", without much reflection, while the individuals nonetheless continue to choose and reject the various options that offer themselves.

The life projects are initially typically concerned with establishing a good family life and a satisfying working life, including possible career ambitions. However, there may also be strong life projects that focus on leisure activities, interests and political, religious or other convictions. If, based on these projects, the individual is able to see the meaning of the learning, adults are actually able to learn amazingly much, and if the subject is one the individual is passionate about acquiring, and receives adequate support for the efforts, learning may also take place at amazing speed.

Illustrations of this are, of course, numerous, because this is something that takes place all the time for most adults: we notice impulses in our everyday lives that we may use in the contexts to which we are committed, while the rest fade away rapidly. If we watch television, for instance the news, something may come up which has a personal significance, and then we acquire the information immediately. The rest we forget very soon, assuming that we took it in the first place.

However, many other examples can be mentioned. The individual who takes an interest in gardening learns much about plants and soil conditions, the computer enthusiast accumulates IT skills, most adults learn to drive a car, some with enthusiasm, others with great difficulty, but they need the skill, and therefore almost eventually all manage it. People who learned to see themselves as miserable at mathematics at school nonetheless learn basic arithmetical skills to manage in their daily lives (Nunes et al. 1993). When we have children, we learn how to nurse and tend them, and many even attend prenatal classes and courses in childcare. Of course, there may be difficulties and blocks, but when there is something we really want to learn, we almost always find a way to do so.

More generally, it may expressed along the lines that adult learning has the character that:

- *adults learn what they want to learn when it is meaningful for them to learn*
- *adults, when learning, draw on the resources they have*
- *adults assume the responsibility for their learning they are interested in taking (provided that they have the opportunity).*
  (according to Illeris 2002, p. 219)

We might reverse these formulations. Then the key message would be that adults have very little inclination to learn something that makes no sense or has no meaning on the basis of their own perspective.

The educational significance is that the learning that adults derive from a programme of education to a very high degree, and a much higher degree than children, depends on the conscious and subconscious motivation they bring to the programme, and how the motivation is met. This motivation is, naturally, not beyond the reach of influence, but outside influence, whether it assumes the form of conversation, guidance, persuasion, pressure or compulsion, will always be received in the light of the individual's own experience and perspectives. If they are to change the possibilities for learning, the influences must be convincing on this basis, i.e. the adults must accept them psychologically, and must be brought to see the meaning with the education programme in question for themselves and their situation.

8.3. Cognitive learning

The discussion of the special character of adult learning in the previous section in relation to such fundamental matters as control, identity and meaning makes it clear that it concerns learning as a whole, i.e. all the three dimensions of learning. At the same time, however, there is an ongoing, important discussion concerning adults' possibilities for learning, especially in the cognitive area.

The cognitive learning theories first developed in the 1930s by the Swiss researcher Jean Piaget and the Russian Lev Vygotsky focused on the development of learning possibilities through the period of childhood, not least Piaget's much debated stage theory, which, on the basis of extensive empirical studies, maintains that there is a highly specific course of development through a number of given cognitive stages and sub-stages (see e.g. Flavell 1963, Vygotsky 1978). However, for Piaget the structural development of learning possibilities ends when a child at the age of 11 to 13 reaches the "formal operational" level, which makes logical-deductive thinking possible. This possibility supplements the forms of thinking and learning. There is, as I see it, no evidence that this involves a new and higher cognitive stage in the sense of Piaget, but the ability of formal operations can through (formal or informal) training and practice be developed in these directions.

Piaget's perception of this has been questioned from several quarters. On the one hand, it has been pointed out that far from all adults are actually able to think formally operationally in the formally logical sense inherent in Piaget's definition. Empirical research shows that in England it is actually less than 30 per cent, but at the same time it confirms that at the beginning of puberty a decisive development takes place in the possibilities for learning and thinking in abstract terms, so that, all in all, distinguishing a new cognitive phase is justified (Shayer & Adey, 1981). On the other hand, it has been maintained that, at a later time, significant new cognitive possibilities that extend beyond the formally operative may develop (e.g. Commons, Richards & Amon, 1984). American adult education researcher Stephen Brookfield has summarised this criticism by pointing out four possibilities for learning which, in his opinion, are only developed in the course of adulthood: the capacity for dialectical thinking, the capacity for applying practical logic, the capacity for realising how one may know what one knows (meta-cognition), and the capacity for critical reflection (Brookfield 2000).

The conclusion of all this must be that in puberty there appears to be a physiological maturing of the central nervous system that makes possible a new form of abstract and stringent thinking and learning, so that an individual becomes able to operate context-independently with coherent concept systems, and that this ability through the ages of youth and adulthood may be developed further in the direction of, inter alia, formal logical, practical logical, dialectical, meta-cognitive and critical reflective thinking and learning.

In the case of young people, we can thus observe a new cognitive capacity that supplements the more concrete thinking and learning of childhood with decisive new possibilities. This new capacity for understanding and acquiring larger conceptual contexts characterises learning motivation to a high degree during the years of youth. Young people are determined to find out how things are structured, and this applies to matters personal, social, scientific, societal, political, religious and metaphysical.

It is thus at one and the same time the longing for independence and the longing for coherent understanding of how they themselves and their environment function and why things are the way they are which, in a decisive way separate adult learning from the learning of childhood. Up through the period of youth, individuals will themselves increasingly assume responsibility for their own learning and non-learning. They will choose and reject, and in this context understand what they are dealing with and their own roles and possibilities. However, all this has been enormously complicated by the duality of late modernity between, on the one hand, the apparently limitless degrees of freedom and reams of information, and, on the other hand, far-reaching indirect pressure for control from parents, teachers, youth cultures, mass media and formal conditions for possibilities. The transition from child to adult has thus, in the area of learning, become an extended, ambiguous and complicated process, with blurred outlines and unclear conditions and goals.

8.4. Learning capacity and age

There is a widespread perception that adults are poorer learners, or at least slower learners than children and young people, and that this is increasingly true the older a person gets. This mode of perception is, however, much too poor on nuances, and most people also know examples of the opposite: that adults in certain situations have acquired some kind of learning or skill both very rapidly and in a highly qualified manner. The latter is connected not least with the fact that adults typically possess a broader and deeper experiential basis than children and young people, that they have more to which they may relate new impulses, and therefore may acquire a broader and more nuanced understanding.

With the perception of the special characteristics of adult learning outlined above, the outline of a basis for understanding this paradox also appears. The decisive key factor concerning adult learning is the question of who controls and determines the learning. When adults are more or less compelled to enter into a learning situation that they have not themselves chosen, certain defence or resistance elements will always, consciously or subconsciously, make their impact felt, thus reducing the speed and quality of the learning. Individuals feel that "their heart is not in it", which weakens their interest and concentration. There are usually plenty of other things to think about and take care of.

However, if the learning has been chosen by the individual, and even more so if it is something the person is passionate about, something of substantial significance for the life projects the person is engaged in, the adult may apply her/himself to the learning with full capacity and a broad experience basis. It is not the capacity there is something wrong with if the learning is slow and arduous, but the motivation that is too weak and the competition with other commitments that is too strong.

One matter of special significance in this context occurs when the adult passes the point in life that the Danish researcher Johan Fjord Jensen has called the "life turn" (Jensen 1993). It is highly individual when this takes place; for most people it happens somewhere between the ages of 45 and 65, for some few perhaps not at all. In its essence, the event consists in the person's not only cognitive but also emotional realisation that one's life span is limited. This experience, which may be slow and gradual or appear suddenly in connection with a watershed event in one's life, has great significance for the learning, i.e in the way in which, consciously or perhaps more often less consciously, the individual may dramatically sharpen the sorting and selection of what to "invest" mental energy in learning. The person becomes less inclined to expend strength on acquiring learning that he/she cannot see the meaning of when constantly bearing in mind that the time available is limited.

Therefore we see, not least at a time when adult learning and lifelong learning encroach on us, that many slightly older adults have major problems, and cause major problems, when they are to participate in educational and retraining activities that they may be forced to take part in, but which they do not wish to attend. With age it becomes increasingly difficult to force oneself to learn something that one does not accept deep down. But we also see other older adults who, for instance, retire on pension or anticipatory pension in order to begin new learning courses which they pursue passionately, because now at long last they have found the opportunity to concentrate on an interest or a challenge of their own choice (cf. Jarvis 2001).

It is as though the opposition between what is pleasurable and what is laborious in the learning are polarised, confronted and resolved in a new and more definitive way among the group of mature and resourceful elder adults who with the life turn reach a final prioritisation of their needs, and thereby become able to realise late modern society's enormous range of options more freely than ever before. This seems to be an infinitely privileged situation. However, in its consistent form, it is presumably even in the most privileged societies only a small minority with good health and sufficient mental and financial resources who reach this point. All the same, the possibility may be a point of reference for learning in mature adults and as a perspective that may further make visible that adult learning is otherwise always trapped in the paradox between freedom and necessity, between power and powerlessness, between individuality and social coherence, as has been pointed out probably most directly by the English education sociologist Peter Jarvis (1992, p. 80).

8.5. Learning strategies

Precisely this paradox may also both generally and in relation to the concrete and current situation in adult education be understood as the background for the observation that adults in a learning context typically more or less consciously practise a number of strategies for their learning. It must be understood as a kind of behaviour that aims to balance both their own ambivalence and the contradictory situation in which they find themselves. In our research we have, among other things, taken part in attempts to discover and understand a number of these strategies as they find expression in the everyday life of education (Illeris 2003a). We found that the strategies unfold at two levels.

First is what might be called an intermediate level, because it is not concerned with the most general matters pertaining to the act of learning as part of the course of one's life, and on the other hand it is not concerned with individual concrete situations either. It is concerned with how one might handle the relationship between the way in which the learning course functions and one's own relationship to the course.

Second is a more concrete level. It is concerned with the ability to live with the daily small and large manifestations of the tendency to outside control and disempowerment which, as described, lies latent in the adult education programmes in all the cases where the adult participant has not undertaken the education programme fully driven by a personal wish and interest. It is especially characteristic at this concrete level that the individual participant does not apply merely one strategy, but in the course of the day applies several different strategies and assumes many different positions.

At the first level, one may in certain cases meet participants with "pure" positive or negative strategies, either concerned with making the most of it at all times or having abandoned all pretence and just not caring at all. Such attitudes are very rare and probably require a degree of clarity that the complicated conditions do not exactly promote. There were, on the other hand, other strategies that we found widely common.

The most positive of these strategies focuses on the effort of the individual participant to find out which elements of the course might be subjectively useful or personally satisfying to acquire, to concentrate on this, and more or less ignore the rest. The elements that are selected are then typically practical skills and knowledge which for the individual might be perceived as useful in everyday life, in working life or with a view to gaining employment. This may, for instance, typically be practical craftsmanship techniques and skills, knowledge and skills within information technology or the acquisition of foreign languages. However, there may also be commitment of a more experiential or enlightening character, e.g. within film, theatre or literature.

The other widespread strategy at this level is the more instrumentally orientated individual, who aims to complete the course as easily as possible, i.e. to figure out what is formally and informally acceptable and then just meet the lowest performance requirements permissible while avoiding trouble. If, for instance, a certain attendance rate is required, e.g. for obtaining formal recognition of participation, the person will make sure to meet the requirement and no more, and generally take part in no more of the activities than what is required to manage, academically and mentally.

At the more concrete level a multitude of more socially orientated strategies flourish, which are often perceived by the teacher as annoying and deviating in relation to the planned programme. This may e.g. be the use of humour and irony, which may provide an outlet for frustrations, insecurity and an experience of inadequacy, and which at the same time may break the monotony, make the situation more tolerable, and which it is difficult for others to relate to in a negative way. It may also be that a person ceaselessly complains, not so seriously that real action must be taken, but perhaps more to while away the time, maintain some sort of self-respect, and challenge "the system" a little bit. A third possibility may be "dynamisation", i.e. throwing oneself into certain elements or activities in the education programme and devoting enormous energy and attention to them in order at least to feel alive and active, more than in order actually to acquire the skills or knowledge. It may also be the perfectionist strategy to pursue certain parts or elements of the programme down to the smallest detail, so the person may achieve a sense of mastery and competence, without it being in any way particularly important or relevant.

As regards learning, the strategies will figure as a defence against the developments and changes which the programmes aim to achieve but which the participants find it difficult to accept. Therefore they also appear as hindrances for the intended learning, but rarely as the more focused resistance that may possibly promote alternative fruitful learning. Generally, the strategies must therefore be considered signs that there is something inappropriate in the situation. Most often this may be an underlying clash or incongruity which ultimately is concerned with matters that the participants have not accepted and perhaps cannot accept, and to which the teacher and the institution are only able to respond in a more or less superficial way, because they are rooted in a more fundamental societal and political conflict.

In this connection, quite a few psychologists and philosophers have referred to the popular concept of wisdom, which is usually ascribed to a chosen few older people. There is certainly no agreement as to what the specific characteristics or criteria of such wisdom are, but it seems in general to be related to life experience and often also to an ability to accept ambiguity and see issues and problems from various perspectives. Sharan Merriam and Rosemary Cafarella conclude an examination of several writings on wisdom with the following statement:

> "Although it has been discussed over the ages by the great philosophers and theologians, this area of study has received little attention in the literature on cognitive development and learning in general. [...] Despite the different perspectives from which wisdom is viewed, scholars seem to agree that wisdom involves special types of experience-based knowledge and is characterized by the ability to move away from absolute truth, to be reflective, and to make sound judgements related to everyday life." (Merriam & Cafarella 1999, p. 167)

9. Different adults learn differently

The previous chapter was about what in general characterises adult learning. This chapter deals with a number of important differences of general significance for learning by different groups of adults. There are four types of differences which are of particular importance: differences with respect to position on the labour market, generation differences, gender differences, and differences to do with ethnicity. In the practice of adult education, these differences are woven into a variegated heterogeneous pattern, often with great variations that can be difficult and challenging to accommodate in a joint course. There are special challenges to adult education programmes on the way with the generation of "new young people", who generally have a quite different attitude to the education situation than that of previous generations at whom these education programmes are mostly aimed.

9.1. The work perspective as point of departure

Both in the ideology of lifelong learning and quite explicitly in the formulation, "lifelong learning for all", lies a clear intention that adult education is to be a broad and popular matter (OECD 1996, cf. chapter 2). The strong expansion in the area in the 1990s has also in many countries included a proliferation of adult education to broader segments of the population, i.a. through initiatives in connection with reducing unemployment.

However, the fact remains that those less used to engaging in education must, as a rule, be in a special situation or receive encouragement to embark on participation in adult education. This special situation is usually attached to the individual's place in relation to the labour market: it becomes necessary to upgrade qualifications to keep one's work, a person has been away from the labour market and must undergo training and education to get a job, a person is or becomes unemployed and is activated through education, rehabilitation, or a person retires on pension or early pension and gets the opportunity for spending time on education.

When one interviews participants in the broad adult education and training programmes in Denmark and asks them about the reason why they are taking an education, one almost always gets an answer that relates to their situation in relation to the labour market, and it is characteristic that the replies fall into two main groups.

On the one hand, there are those who have work or are completing an education that provides professional qualifications. They are, as a rule, very focused and at the same time typically rather narrow in their perspective; they want to learn what is necessary, what it takes to pass a certain test, or what is immediately applicable in their job. Everything else is usually perceived as a waste of time or as less interesting.

On the other hand, there are the unemployed. They are, as a rule, unambiguously governed by a wish to get work, any work that they can handle, but they do not know what they can get, so they are less directly focused, more searching and more accepting towards a broader and more general qualification.

Also for those with a higher education, the participation in adult education is, as a rule, first and foremost related to their employment situation. This applies e.g. typically to management training or professional supplementary training, but it may also be a more general upgrading, e.g. in a foreign language. Almost all adult education for those who already have a higher education has, to a greater or lesser degree, a career perspective and is thereby also, in another way than for most of the less educated, self-chosen and focused, or else it is indirectly labour market related in the sense that the student is withdrawing from the labour market and would like to take up some interests that the student has not up to that point found the time and energy to manage (cf. Jarvis 2001).

It is thus characteristic that adult education and training participants first and foremost, but in many different ways, relate their education situation to their situation in relation to the labour market, and that their relation to the education they are taking, the way they generally experience and handle it, is also linked to the relationship to the labour market. The line of separation between those who are in or experience that they are entering, those who are out and cannot see a certain or just a likely way in, and the third group, who are out or on their way out and do not wish to return, turns out to be the most fundamental element of the way in which participants experience the education, and how they relate to what takes place in the education.

There is today a close relationship between the overall administration of adult education programmes and the attitude the participants display: both levels are predominantly determined by labour market policy. Plans are made on the basis of the relations to the labour market, and other matters are assessed from that point of departure also.

However, what this means in concrete terms at the personal level can be very different for the different participants. It is closely attached to their life situation, their life story and their life perspectives. For the decidedly career-oriented or leisure-oriented, the situation is basically quite simple: they have a goal with their education, pursue this goal to the extent they can handle it, and can become irritated or disappointed if the education fails to live up to their expectations. However, for most participants in the broad adult education programmes things are different. Their situation is in different ways more ambiguous and forms part of a more complicated interplay with their life situation and interests, and this finds expression in various ways, which besides the relationship to the labour market especially relates to age and gender.

The material of the Danish research in which I have been engaged distinguishes clearly three generations of participants, who generally relate very differently to adult education programmes, and at least within the two oldest generations also some typical gender differences are manifested (Illeris 2003a). In the following sections, I shall take the three generations as my point of departure, and consider the gender differences within each of the generations.

9.2. Wage-earner identity in the oldest generation

The oldest generation of the participants in the broad adult education programmes are typically from 45 to 50 years old and up, but the limit is of course vague when considered according to age, and characteristics that are marked with the oldest generation can to some extent also be found in the younger generations in less marked forms.

The attitude of the oldest generation is generally dominated by the fundamental identity form that has been called wage-earner consciousness, wage-earner lifestyle or wage-earner identity (Popitz et al. 1957). The core of this identity form is that wage-work is perceived as the necessary and unavoidable basis of life. As a wage earner, one must conform and do what others have determined within the working hours. In return, one receives wages that one can spend on creating one's own life during the free time.

In the classical wage-earner consciousness, the worker is thus fundamentally a subordinate, forced to work on other people's premises to maintain her/his existence. The attitude to work is essentially instrumental, work is the means to maintain existence, ultimately a necessary evil, an exploitation that one must resign to and bear. In order to achieve the best possible conditions for this work, workers must unite, show solidarity, organise and fight for their rights. They have a dichotomised picture of the social universe, divided between "those up there" who decide, and "us down here" who must supply the work on which society ultimately rests.

In extension of this, the attitude towards education is also fundamentally instrumental. The necessary qualifications are something to be acquired, either through a basic trade education or directly through one's work. Work-related education beyond this is only meaningful if there is an unambiguous need for new qualifications which cannot be acquired through work. As a point of departure, this generation perceives education as something unwanted, in some cases actually humiliating, for if one has to take an education it must be because one is not good enough as one is.

In the course of the education itself they want immediately clear goals and rules. It should preferably be like attending school, and learning is something that takes place when one is taught. The teacher is therefore placed in a role along the line of the employer or the foreman, as those who have the power and right to decide, those who have the responsibility and know how things must be done; but the power and right are only in force during the determined tuition time and not one second longer. They only assume responsibility for being there on time and do as they are told, and if the teacher attempts something else, e.g. more participant-directed forms of learning, they are on guard and resist, at least until they have been otherwise convinced (Illeris 2000, 2003a).

In our research, we have as mentioned found that adult education participants who (in 1998-99) were over 45-50 years, typically were fundamentally bearers of such a wage-earner identity and related to the education on this basis.

Generally we may first and foremost characterise them as unequivocally work-oriented in the sense that all matters in connection with education are assessed based on their relevance in relation to the participants' perception of their work or the work they may hope to get. Furthermore, they may typically be characterised as stable and loyal to authority within the given framework. They come when they must and do what they are told, usually without questions asked or taking a personal position, as long as they perceive the activities to be legitimate, i.e. immediately work-relevant. The teacher is viewed in relation to the education as the one who knows everything and masters everything that is relevant, the one who has the ability and must direct and decide what is to be done, and the one who is able to judge whether participants got things right or wrong.

Furthermore, in this generation we have found an obvious gender difference in the sense that the men typically have been more limited and rule-oriented, while the women have been more conforming, accepting and sometimes even thankful in relation to the teacher and the education situation generally. The men have been oriented towards doing what they must, but certainly no more than that, and even though they have related to the teacher as an authority, they have also emphasised equality at the human level. The women have been more oriented towards making the best of it and have often conformed and subjected themselves, and in some cases been virtually admiring towards their teachers.

As concerns the "soft" or personal qualifications that form part of the modern concept of competence, this generation finds it difficult to understand and accept what these things are really about in more than a superficial and external way. The men have a tendency to reinterpret the soft personal qualities as certain external patterns of behaviour, while the women apparently take these matters more to heart, however, without this becoming more than kindness and figures of speech. It is not part of the paid-employment relationship to sell one's personality, soul or identity, only one's labour, and this fundamental attitude is carried over also into education, at any rate until practice possibly shows that the situation might be different here.

9.3. The more floating wage-earner identity in the middle generation

The middle generation typically spans the age bracket from the 25-30 year olds up to the 45-50 year-olds, i.e. by far the largest part of the participants in broad adult education programmes, and those at whom the effort in the area is also first and foremost directed. Both downwards and upwards the limit may be fairly floating, both as concerns the actual age and as concerns the features and characteristics that are included in the descriptions.

The middle generation also fundamentally holds a wage-earner identity, but it is less sharp in its outline and is to varying degrees diffused by development trends that have arisen in step with the development of the welfare society. A Danish project, which draws a profile of union members at the beginning of the 1990s, describes this as developments from a classic material and collectivist value orientation in the direction towards a more non-material and more individualistic orientation. This produces a trend containing a picture of four indistinctly defined and partly overlapping wage-earner types, who are characterised as the welfare worker (material and collectivist), the salaried employee (non-material and collectivist), the liberalist (material and individualistic), and the careerist (non-material and individualistic) (Bild et al. 1993).

In our research we have not worked with such a typology, but in the middle generation we have in many ways been able to observe indications of a softening in relation to the classical wage-earner identity. First and foremost there is an indication of a more accepting attitude towards education generally. Among the middle generation it is not in any way personally or socially humiliating for an adult to have to undergo education and training. However, it is not a matter of course and, as a rule, not something one wishes for. Members of this group still have a view that education primarily belongs to childhood and youth, but they are also ready to accept that for many it can be necessary with an upgrade or new qualifications as an adult, and when they find themselves in the situation, they must turn up and make the most of it.

This takes place in innumerable different ways, in which it is highly varying what is left of the classical wage-earner attitude; e.g. one can observe some clear gender differences where the men are typically more individualistic and performance oriented, while the women are more collectivist and cooperation oriented. Furthermore, the men are as a rule strongly oriented towards the professional contents of the education programmes, which are considered the very point and something that is not to be questioned, it is what must be learned; while the women are typically more ambivalent, both in a tension between the professional and the social elements, and more generally between the education and the parent and/or housewife role which at the same time makes its impact felt (cf. Becker-Schmidt 1987).

In relation to the "soft" or personal qualifications, the attitude among the middle generation is quite clearly that education is primarily concerned with the "hard" qualifications, i.e. the professional contents, but they are not dismissive or clueless like the oldest generation towards a simultaneous orientation towards the personal dimension. They understand what it is all about, they would in a way like to include it, but they are uncertain towards it and probably do not really believe in it. As a point of departure, education is "attending school" like they did as children, and it takes a major and convincing effort on the part of the teacher for learning to be anything else (Illeris 2003a).

Not least in this context there are typical features which the middle generation seem to carry with them from their school days into adult education: it is often quite remarkable, at times verging on sheer comedy, how adult males in adult education programmes so to speak transmogrify themselves into children and begin acting like "naughty boys" who talk in class, provoke the teacher, compete for being the naughtiest and wittiest, and even begin shooting paper bullets, and similar. The women actually often also metamorphose into children, but then typically in the direction of the role as the "good girls" who submit themselves, over-fulfil what they perceive as the teacher's aims, and with demonstrative displays of self-righteous indignation assume the role of the teacher's lieutenants when "the boys" must be called to order.

In terms of education and pedagogy, the middle generation thus behave as a highly heterogeneous group, which still share the common feature that they basically accept the education situation and orient themselves towards the immediate professional relevance, which they perceive as being virtually identical with the professional qualification. There is, however, as a rule no immediate orientation towards personal development, and emphasis on the part of the teacher in this area requires extensive and very well structured efforts. As mentioned earlier, the unemployed are more inclined to accept the inclusion of the personal dimension than those who are in, or have prospects of, regular employment.

9.4. The young generation

The most profound separation between the participating generations in broad adult education programmes is, however, the division between the youngest generation, the new young people on their way to becoming the new adults (Simonsen 2000), and the two older generations. The age limit is of course also here floating, but it is quite marked: the individual participant belongs mentally, as a rule, quite obviously to either the middle or the youngest generation. In 1998-99, in Denmark the divide was typically located around the mid-20s, and there were therefore still relatively few participants from the youngest generation in the courses we observed in our research. Among the persons we interviewed there was, among other, a then 31-year-old man, who clearly belonged to the new generation, but also a 25-year-old who equally obviously belonged to the middle generation (Illeris 2003a).

The young generation are generally strongly influenced by the cultural and social landslide which i.a. has been called "the cultural liberation" (e.g. Ziehe & Stubenrauch 1982, Simonsen 2000), "late-modernity" (e.g. Giddens 1990, 1991) or "post-modernity" (e.g. Usher et al. 1997, Usher 1998, 2000). Culturally viewed this includes a dissolution or relativisation of traditional structures, norms and attitudes that on the one hand have liberated the individual from the ties and limitations of earlier times, and simultaneously have confronted the individual with the necessity of having to choose and shape lifestyle, biography and identity in a universe with possibilities that are apparently almost infinite. Socially considered, this includes i.a. the emergence and penetration of information technology, globalisation and the market society.

For this generation, education is not merely something concerned with qualification, but at the same time, and more fundamentally, it is a core element in the constant identity developments that have always characterised youth, but now seem to be able to drag out indefinitely, or at any rate extend a searching and non-committal youth period far into the 30s. Young people are therefore also not so focused on working life: receiving public welfare or getting by on temporary, part-time jobs is quite acceptable and they have a "let's-try-it" and consumer-oriented attitude towards different education offers. They are entirely prepared to accept lifelong learning and education as part of their constant identity development and metamorphosis, but at the same time they relate everything the education programmes offer directly to their own current needs and projects, and if they do not perceive what is being taught as relevant and personally rewarding they drop out, either directly by abandoning their education, by being absent, or mentally by reducing their commitment (cf. e.g. Simonsen 2000).

Teachers typically experience these new young adults as apparently first and foremost self-centred and demanding, often unreasonably so. They can be difficult; both because they insist on receiving individual attention, that the teacher must relate to them as persons, not just as students or participants, and because they do not just do as they are told. However, if the situation is viewed from their perspective, these very features are wholly necessary for the education to be able to contribute to their identity development process, which is after all an individual matter. Teachers can perceive them as both unruly and irresponsible, but on the basis of their own perspectives and premises, they are rather autonomous and far more responsible than their elders, who allow the teacher and the subject and the teaching plan decide. They do precisely assume responsibility for their own learning, but in the way that they only want to learn what they themselves think that they can use for something (Simonsen 2000, Illeris 2003e).

In the coming years, this new generation will start filling an ever increasing volume of participants in adult education programmes and challenge their flexibility and tolerance fundamentally. As it has already happened in Danish youth education programmes, there will be tension and eruptions, and in adult education programmes there will not only be clashes with established systems, institutions and teachers, but doubtlessly also with the older generations of adult participants. There may be some exciting pedagogical perspectives in this which education programmes and educators must attempt to cultivate and fertilise.

9.5. Ethnicity

The descriptions above have clearly related to education participants with a background that is culturally in line with Danish traditions. However, many countries also see the entry of more and more participants with another ethnic background than the national culture into the ordinary adult education programmes, and their way of experiencing and relating to adult education may in many ways be very different.

At the special courses for immigrants these matters naturally stand at the centre, and have already to a considerable extent led to the development of special pedagogical approaches, which i.a. take their basis in the different participant groups' cultural and educational background and ways of understanding.

However, there are also rising numbers of participants with another ethnic background than the national culture in the ordinary adult education programmes, and this can to a high degree complicate the situation even more, because then other and mutually very different backgrounds interact with the already complicated patterns in the ethnically national participants' prior qualifications and attitudes.

This entire issue will not be addressed here, partly because it is so many-sided and complicated, partly because there is not sufficient research on the area. However, it is clear that it can only add further to the necessity for an orientation towards the premises, interests, ambivalences, defence and resistance potential at play in the broad adult education programmes today.

In a number of cases, another ethnic background will involve an approach to education that is immediately more loyal towards authority and submissive. As concerns learning and not least competence development, such obedience to authority can be problematic, and the orientation towards the participants' prior qualifications will also involve consideration and development of approaches that can loosen this obedience to authority. Still more, this points towards the duality of a teacher direction that aims at a participant direction which increasingly emerges as a fundamental condition for the role as adult teacher. I shall return to this in the third part of the book.

9.6. The heterogeneous participant backgrounds

As a whole, it is important to maintain that there are very large differences between different groups of participants in the broad adult education programmes, not just with regard to the academic prior qualifications, but far more profound in relation to the perception of what education is generally all about, what it can be used for, and how one experiences and relates to being involved in education.

For the two oldest generations, two fundamental matters are very important and characteristic: first, that education is predominantly considered in relation to the working life and the situation of the individual in relation to the labour market, that it is concerned with acquiring of the immediately applicable professional qualifications; second, that education is in principle something that belongs to childhood and youth and it is not immediately experienced as "proper" for an adult to have to "go back to school". Besides this, there are some significant differences between the oldest generations' less flexible attitudes towards education and the middle generation's more open and accepting attitudes, and between men's more one-sided orientation towards contents and women's more social orientation.

However, for the youngest participant generation which only in these years are in earnest entering adult education programmes – where professional/academic and the personal elements are closely integrated – the employment orientation is weaker and only one part of the personal identity project. For the young adults this is at the same time the core of their orientation towards and acceptance of lifelong learning as a condition of existence. In a certain way, the attitudes of the young adults are closer to more career-oriented attitudes in slightly older and often previously higher educated adults' approach. The clear difference is that where the career-oriented as a rule are very focused, the young adults are in their point of departure searching, and focus only enters if they are "turned on" by the education course in question.

The very large and profound differences between different large participant groups mean that adult education programmes must of necessity be manifold and highly diverse, and the development around the new generation will add further complication to the situation. There is thus a clear need for a broad general appeal and avoidance of uniformity in the range of adult education programmes offered, but also within the individual education and in each individual class the differences will of necessity make themselves felt and place great demands on both the flexibility of the framework and on the teachers and their structuring and execution of the education activities.

Through modern concepts like goal and frame management and similar instruments, institutions have apparently regarded diversity and differences, but other current initiatives demand for uniform levels, taximeter schemes and evaluations pull in the opposite direction. Out there at the institutions, there are routines, traditions and school cultures which also have a constricting effect on the necessary variation and flexibility. If the ideal of lifelong learning and the need for a broad and flexible competence development are to have a real opportunity in practice, adult education programmes must, not only on paper but also in reality, socially and psychologically, be able to contain and accommodate the great differences among the participants. The growing share of the new generation in the total picture will increasingly sharpen these challenges.

10. The contexts of learning

Learning always takes place in a certain context and courses of learning are embedded in different kinds of framework conditions. Four types of framework conditions are taken up in this chapter: institutionalised learning that takes place in schools and other educational institutions; everyday learning that takes place in the many and varied contexts of "spare time"; the learning of working life that takes place in connection with one's place of work; and, virtual learning via the computer and IT. Each of these "set-ups" has certain advantages and disadvantages that must be considered. In many cases the optimum would be a combination that is tailor-made with a view to the intended learning of a specific group of participants.

10.1. Situated learning

General differences in the learning depend not only on the learners' different social and personal position in various dimensions, such as employment, age and gender, but also on the context in which the learning takes place. This is so because the relationship which the learner has to the learning context will always have an impact on the learning, on several levels even: in schooling e.g. typically in relation to the teacher, to comrades, to the subject, to the school in question and generally to attending school. It is especially this latter level I shall deal with here. What does it mean for the learning whether it takes place in an educational institution, in a general practice context, in the workplace, or perhaps computer-mediated in a virtual space?

In connection with the significance of the framework conditions and situations for the learning, it is obvious to refer to the concept of "situated learning", which, among other things on the basis of experience with apprenticeship-like learning traditions in non-industrialised countries, has been developed in America by the anthropologist Jean Lave, partly in co-operation with the psychologist Etienne Wenger, and which in recent years has gained widespread acceptance, also in Europe (Lave & Wenger 1991).

On the face of it, situated learning appears as a general concept that states that all learning takes place in a specific situation, and that this situation is of significance for the character of the learning and its result. Thus, Lave and Wenger write that the concept

> *"took on the proportions of a general theoretical perspective, the basis of claims about the relational character of knowledge and learning, about the negotiated character of meaning, and about the concerned (engaged, dilemma-driven) nature of learning activity for the people involved. That perspective meant that there is no activity that is not situated." (Lave & Wenger 1991, p. 33)*

According to Lave and Wenger, it is not only that the specific situation influences the learning that takes place, but it also has an influence on what already developed learning results are activated. When the learning takes place in interaction between the already developed structures and new impulses, the environment and the learning situation thus influence not only the learner's perception of the new impulses, but also the already developed structures that are involved in the inner adaptation processes (cf. section 6.3).

However, it is as though Lave and Wenger in their book give the concept a special twist, for their central message is not that all learning is influenced by the situation in which it takes place, but rather that a certain type of situations have some specific learning qualities, i.e. situations that the authors generally term legitimate peripheral participation in a community of practice. This occurs e.g. typically in apprenticeships in an enterprise, whereas what takes place in a formalised education programme is not considered a community of practice and is therefore not treated as situated learning (see also Illeris 2002, chapter 10). The decisive issue in this terminology is thus whether the learning is situated in the same context as the one in which it is to be applied.

However, for present purposes I shall adhere to fundamentals, i.e. that learning is always influenced by the situation in which it takes place, and take a closer look at adult learning in formalised education, in voluntary communities of practice, in workplaces or virtually through computer mediation.

10.2. Adult learning in formalised education

As considered in the previous chapter, the point of departure for adults' participation in formalised education is typically characterised by the feature that, in a certain and often difficult and challenging personal situation, they more or less voluntarily or of necessity choose or are referred to an education programme towards which they are to some extent ambivalent. They hope sincerely that the programme will be able to help them, but are at the same time sceptical as to whether any benefits will materialise and what it will do to them.

These education courses take place within the framework of some institutions that have physical facilities, staff hired to handle various functions, rules and provisions regulating what is to take place, and traditions, self-perceptions and an institutional culture that determines the practice.

Generally it might be said that this is *institutionalised* education and learning. The institutions and their activities are society's offer and represent at the same time society's demands which the participants are faced with. The participants' own personal and social situation means that in most cases they want to or have to get an education or training, and in many cases the situation also points towards specific education programmes as the relevant or directly imposed options. Inherent in this is that the situation is generally institutionalised; the adults in question may, as a rule, not resolve it freely in accordance with their own wishes. The solution must be found within some institutionalised framework over which they have little or no influence.

The learning that is supposed to take place and that the participants in their own ways hope for, is bound to the framework within which it is to unfold: it becomes what the participants to a greater or lesser extent perceive as "school learning". This perception means not merely that the learning is influenced by the norms of the school, its values, views and perceptions, but also that it can often be difficult to understand entirely what it is meant to be used for and therefore also to use it or recall it outside the school setting.

The participants "know" this in one way or another, and so do all the other people involved, i.e. instructors, administrators, counsellors, caseworkers, etc. They also all know that school learning perhaps is not what best corresponds to the participants' needs. It is a significant part of the background for the participants' ambivalent attitudes to the education programmes, and, as a rule, all the other actors involved have an understanding of this. However, these are all matters that are seldom discussed, for society has no immediately available alternative offers other than institutionalised initiatives, and this would usually mean some or other form of school attendance.

The schools or institutions that constitute options have, of course, been developed with a view to handling the kind of tasks they are facing, e.g. a certain type of adult education. Usually, however, they have been set up at an earlier point in time when the needs were not quite the same, and have then been adapted and updated. At the same time the schools have recorded their own history and developed rules and traditions. The instructors and other staff add their personal character. Therefore, the outcome may to a certain extent be different and fit to different degrees the current challenges, but there will always be an attempt to unite the current challenges with the conditions produced by the historical development of the institution in question.

In some cases, e.g. typically in vocationally orientated education programmes, educators have tried to a considerable extent to alleviate the undesirable aspects of school learning by creating a school environment that is very similar to the conditions that obtain in the trade that the education programmes aim to prepare students for; schools have developed what I have previously, with others, characterised as a "vocationally oriented school environment" (Andersen & Illeris, 1995, cf. section 11.4). The participants in these education programmes accept this to a high degree, and it presumably also reduces the problems involved in the transition between school and working life. However, it may also involve the drawback that participants are not really able or willing to realise that these education programmes *are* school courses, and it may cause some problems because seven to eight hours of school attendance per day is very taxing if practical activities do not constitute a substantial part of the programme.

In other adult education programmes, especially of a more general character, we found the school environment mere directly "school oriented" (Andersen & Illeris 1995, cf. section 11.4). This offers the immediate advantage that the participants find it relatively easy to orientate themselves in relation to it, because it is relatively similar to the conditions they know from their previous school attendance. However, at the same time this poses the obvious risk that the participants are "studentified" or "studentify" themselves, i.e. that they assume a dependent and subject attitude, which clearly makes the learning into school learning to a higher degree than is desirable. This is contrary to the side of adult learning that aims towards development of personal qualifications like flexibility, adaptability, independence, creativity, etc. Educators then attempt to counter this by a direct appeal to the participants, sometimes, as mentioned earlier, almost as a kind of mantra, "We *are* adults, aren't we?"

At the Danish day high schools, much has been done in the tradition of public enlightenment to make the environment "participant oriented" (Andersen & Illeris, 1995, cf. section 11.4), but this can be difficult when the participants are ambivalent because they have not wanted to be in a situation where there is a need for adult education. It can therefore often be problematic to develop and define a clear understanding of participant direction: the participants must, after all, somehow be helped and supported while at the same time they are to decide as much as possible for themselves.

In other adult education programmes at a higher level, e.g. various supplementary education, leadership training or personal development courses, the situation is somewhat different. The participants, as a rule, to a much higher degree have chosen and desired to join the programme in question. In some cases, co-determination is largely limited to this choice, and then participants must accept the degree of "schoolification" inherent in the course. For courses with clearly defined contents, e.g. professional supplementary training courses, this is often accepted even though it is not always particularly felicitous. From the point of view of learning, precisely where the course deals with a subject or professional area with which the participants are already familiar and with which they have practical experience, there is a highly suitable point of departure for participant-directed activities. For courses aiming more at personal development, the "schoolification" is, as a rule, more limited because it is rather obvious that it does not promote such a development. All the same, there may, both on the part of the institutions and the participants, be many features of traditional school attendance that persist, because all in their point of departure have absorbed some habits and perceptions of what one is to do in education programmes. It usually requires a conscious effort to do away with such habits and perceptions.

Generally and across professional areas and levels, the greatest problem for the institutionalised adult education programmes today is that precisely by virtue of being institutionalised programmes they are fundamentally geared for promoting the participants' development of qualifications in a more traditional sense. It is uncertain to what degree that which we usually understand as education is at all suitable for promoting forms of learning that produce the types of competence that are of decisive importance in late modern society (see chapter 3).

When the aims of the processes to a great extent become concerned with personal competences or abilities like flexibility, creativity, independence, service-mindedness, ability to co-operate, responsibility, adaptability, openness and ability to learn more, the entirely fundamental question of whether the education concept which industrial society has produced is at all expedient makes its tremors felt. Flexibility or other corresponding abilities are, after all, not something that can be placed on the school timetable, be taught in the traditional manner or measured in examinations. Conversely, learning and mastery of the facts and skills included in a curriculum seldom guarantee that an individual also has the ability to adapt and apply these qualifications in new and often unpredictable contexts.

Therefore, recent years have seen the rise of fundamental doubts concerning what education in its more or less traditional sense may be used for at all in the society currently developing. A first response has been to attempt to modernise education programmes, e.g. though increased use of project work, teaching differentiation and other more recent pedagogical concepts; I shall return to this in the third part of this book. But is this enough? Perhaps something more radical is needed. It is, at any rate, the key reason why a rapidly growing interest in non-institutionalised learning opportunities outside the education system has emerged in recent years.

Practice learning is becoming a key concept, and therefore it must be dealt with briefly below, even though this book first and foremost is concerned with learning in the formalised adult education programmes.

10.3. Practice learning and everyday learning

The concept of practice learning is used here generally with reference to all learning that takes place in non-institutionalised contexts. We may here again distinguish between two main types. On the one hand is practice learning in regulated contexts, including e.g. learning in workplaces and in associations. On the other hand is the entirely unregulated practice learning that takes place in the many and varied contexts of everyday life, and which is therefore also termed "everyday learning". This distinction corresponds largely to a distinction between "non-formal" and "informal learning" in the more recent, bureaucracy-produced lifelong learning literature, and may be combined with a distinction between intended and incidental learning (cf. e.g. Garrick 1998, Colley et al. 2003).

Everyday learning, then, is the learning that takes place in all the private and non-organised contexts of everyday life. It is most often of a random character, but one may also decide on a more focused effort to learn, e.g. by looking up topics in a work of reference or more systematically by familiarising oneself with something: how an internal combustion engine functions, how to cook Chinese food, or whatever, e.g. by studying handbooks and through conversations, perhaps in a group. And even though the contents are here the centre of attention, the psychodynamic and social dimensions of learning will also be involved (see section 6.2).

Everyday learning naturally has great importance in many contexts; if we were able to quantify learning, it would perhaps amount to as much or more than institutionalised learning. However, even though it may be intentional and focused for the individual, it will, societally, always appear as random, precisely in the sense that it is in no manner regulated, and it cannot be controlled or inspected.

Therefore it is also the background for a societal issue that has attracted much attention in recent years. There is, after all, a wish to acknowledge and use the competences people actually have, but if their competences have been developed through informal everyday learning, no documentation is available. Therefore extensive work is being done to find out how to measure, approve and register people's "real competence" through various forms of "assessment of prior learning" (APL, e.g. Bjørnåvold 2000), an activity of special significance in a number of third world countries, where the formal education system is still only being developed.

10.4. Learning in working life

There seems, however, to have been even greater interest in recent years in the practice learning that takes place at or in connection with work (cf. Illeris, 2003c). An important basis for this interest lies in the perception of situated learning in the above-mentioned book by Lave and Wenger (1991) and Etienne Wenger's later book on communities of practice (Wenger 1998).

It seems obvious that at least three key parties have a considerable interest in moving substantial elements of learning and education from the institutions to working life.

1. Enterprises, public as well as private, will in this way be able better to ensure that employees learn exactly what they need from management's perspective and avoid wasting time on learning which, from this perspective, is unnecessary.
2. The participants will be able to avoid "going back to school again". Learning in working life is not at all perceived as disempowerment in the same way, the use is immediately apparent, learners are not perceived as students but as employees upgrading their skills, and if the learning does not take place in the workplace itself, it is often con-

ducted at training facilities with considerably greater comfort and prestige than ordinary schools and educational institutions.

3. The government has the most obvious interest in thus trying to transfer heavy expenditures for education from the public to the private economy, i.e. paid for by the enterprises or the participants.

Considerable problems are also involved in such a development, which are quite well known, but which currently seem to be fading into the background.

If the learning takes place in working life and on enterprises' terms, that which employers perceive as a desirable focus might easily become a narrowness of the qualification that pursues short-term corporate goals and therefore neglects the more versatile, broad orientation and theoretically qualified competence development that is in the common long-term interest of the participants, society, and ultimately also of enterprises.

In addition, there is a risk that only as few as possible, and primarily those who are already the best qualified groups of employees, will take part in the competence development because the enterprises are of the opinion that this will maximise the fastest returns on their educational investments.

Finally, there is a huge capacity problem. Enterprises in many countries are not able to provide the required capacity for the current apprenticeship and internship schemes as it is, and many enterprises refrain entirely from accepting apprentices and trainees because it complicates work and takes time from the regular employees.

This all adds up to an extensive practical and economic problem. If a significant part of competence development is to take place in the context of working life, there must be a profound change in enterprises' attitudes towards entering into this work in a qualified, open and responsible manner and contributing human, material and financial resources of an entirely different magnitude than previously seen (see e.g. Billett 2001).

It is inherent in this matter that especially small and medium-sized enterprises without an independent personnel function are not immediately prepared to expend more practical and financial resources than necessary on employee training, and some countries have considered it a public sector responsibility to provide ready-made, qualified manpower.

The new demands for competence will no doubt change this tradition considerably, and it will probably to an increasing degree be interesting and profitable for many enterprises, not least within the service and communications areas. However, first, a rather profound and comprehensive change of mentality must take place, and if the scenario is to be realised along a broad front, enterprises must be willing to make a whole-hearted effort and pay what it costs. In addition, there will no doubt be a large group of small enterprises that are neither able nor willing to make the commitment.

All these problems might perhaps then be avoided by choosing a third way on which many pin great hopes, i.e. virtual, computer-mediated learning.

10.5. Virtual learning

Right from the time when "programmed learning" started appearing in the 1960s, many quarters have attached great interest and great expectations for a high volume of learning activity to be mediated through ICT (information and communication technology) (see e.g. Dirckinck-Holm-feld & Fibiger 2002).

When these possibilities emerged, learning was still predominantly perceived in the traditional sense of transfer of facts and information on a given subject, and it was the opinion that doing so through computer programmes would partly save considerable expenditures for instructors and schools, and partly enable the system to secure high and uniform quality.

Nevertheless, it did not become the big hit that some had expected. For even though the software programs were eventually developed and refined, they remained subject to the conditions of impersonal one-way communication, while at the same time development and updating of software programs turned out to be a task of considerable magnitude, also in financial terms. The impact was in practice rather limited, but for concrete information, instruction, etc., there were at least some obvious possibilities in the new medium, and even today the greater part of the computer-mediated learning activities in Denmark assume this form (Elkjær, 2002).

With the emergence of the new demands for competence development it is, however, clear that such a learning approach will only be able to solve very limited tasks; development of personal skills cannot take place through impersonal instruction. Meanwhile, there has been quite considerable technological development, and today there is extensive development work concentrated on the so-called CSCL paradigm (computer-supported collaborative learning), i.e. project work in groups where computer conferences are used in running academic co-operation between the participants and an instructor and among the participants themselves, to various degrees combined with group meetings in which participants get acquainted, receive academic input and can conduct the overall planning and co-ordination of the work of the group.

The specific future perspectives reach further forward towards proper "virtual learning environments" (inter alia with reference to Etienne Wenger's aforementioned concept of communities of practice, Wenger 1998), in which also audio-visual media are used, i.e. the possibility of having conversation and seeing the interlocutor even in distance learning.

These advances open possibilities for virtual learning that may, as concerns personal communication, be impeded by the computer mediation, but on the other hand offers some clear advantages compared to traditional institutionalised education programmes. First, the independence of time and place offers enormous flexibility, which to many adults is of key importance; participants are able to take part in the work irrespective of physical location and residence without leaving home and at the times when it is most convenient. Second, the fact that the communication is written and staggered in time to a higher degree than the direct dialogue seems to challenge participants to reflect and show higher precision in their contributions to the collaborative process.

In this connection it must, however, at the same time be pointed out that the virtual communication requires a considerable measure of motivation and determination to participate to a degree which is far from always present. It is apparently easier to turn up at a school and take part in the direct dialogue than having to muster the self-discipline to work on the computer in the solitude of one's home.

10.6. Interplay

In the above, I have considered four significant "situations" of learning activities: in institutions, in everyday life, in working life and computer-mediated through virtual processes, respectively. Each of these situations has some strengths and weaknesses, as described in brief outlines. It would seem at first glance ideal if the various options could be combined in various formations and with different weighting, in accordance with the relevant type of learning in question.

This is, however, a field that is still relatively new. There is not much experience to draw on, unless we were to consider experience gained from the traditional so-called alternance training programmes, in which there is alternation between periods at school and internships or practice periods. However, it is well known that one of the most often repeated points of criticism levelled against these programmes is that the interplay between the schools and the workplaces is not particularly good. It will take something more, in the shape of an active and co-ordinated inter-play, and again: the will and the resources must be there.

Nonetheless, the interplay between various educational environments is without doubt one of the areas where we find the best opportunities for getting real competence development going, and therefore it is also at this time an important area of efforts for research and development.

Part 3

The practice of adult education programmes

The third part of the book deals with a number of general matters in adult education practice, from the quite overall structures, frames and modes of functioning to general matters to do with the programmes' organisation and implementation and the counselling that is offered.

It is important to emphasise that it is not the business of the book to enter into more specific matters concerning adult education organisation and implementation. On the contrary, it is my position that all these varied and very different issues should be dealt with as closely as possible to the staff and participants involved, because dealing with them is to a wide extent linked to what the individual programme is about and is aiming at and the qualifications, interests and problems that the participants have at the outset.

The point of departure for dealing with the practice of adult education programmes is taken in the general conclusions about their societal functions and the participants' ways of learning from parts 1 and 2, respectively. In extension of this, there is an examination of the question of the division of responsibility between the institutions/teachers and participants as a general and crucial matter of fundamental importance for the nature of the practice that can be realised.

On this basis, the programmes' formal frames, school culture and learning environment, the organisation of the educational activities and a number of crosscutting issues to do with the implementation of the education programmes are examined: the functions of the teachers, division of responsibility in practice, sense of security, challenge, activity, feeling of community and individuality, reflection and reflexivity, monitoring and evaluation

The last chapter in this part is a brief discussion of matters to do with referral, counselling and the way the participants are received at the educational institutions.

11. The basic principles

Taking a starting point in the conclusions of the first and second parts of the book, this chapter discusses the elaboration of the basic principles of adult education programmes, i.e. the fundamental perception of the general objectives of adult education and the way in which these objectives can be translated into framework conditions for practice. There is crucial emphasis on the adult participant being regarded and treated as an independent and responsible person. It is not the task of adult education to take responsibility for the participants' learning but to help them to take on this responsibility themselves, and this attitude must permeate the formal frames, the school culture, the learning environment and the daily practice of adult education. Profound changes are necessary to realise this, on both the formal and the mental level, and such changes must be regarded central to achieving the engagement that is a precondition for effective learning and appropriate competence development.

11.1. Objective perspectives and participants' background

The first part of the book, dealing with the current place and function in society of adult education concluded with drawing up a double general objective perspective with *development of competence and resistancy* as the overall aims and a detailed specification in terms of objectives concerning *overview, orientation towards surrounding world, competence to choose and to act, reflection, reflectivity, critical thinking, self-containment, cooperation, collectivity and social responsibility* (chapter 5).

In relation to the second part of the book, dealing with adults' attitudes towards learning and adult education, it may, in a similar way, be maintained that adults' learning in our current society is fundamentally *selective* and guided by what is perceived as *meaningful* on the basis of the individual's prior learning, situation and future perspectives. Furthermore, it is important that adults' attitudes towards participating in adult education, as a correlative to the above observation, are typically characterised by *ambivalence*, including i.a. an experience of *being returned to a child's role* and *submission,* which is a contradiction of the ideal of being an adult and a self-governing member of a democratic society.

It is thus given these basic premises that adult education programmes must structure and implement learning. It must here be noted that the adults do not react with ambivalence because they are fundamentally against the general perspectives and goals here stated, but because, in specific terms, they experience that they more or less directly have been "placed" in the education programmes in question without having had the opportunity to make a positive choice to participate in them. Because of this, they experience that in the education programmes they are being cast in a student role which is incongruous with feeling like a responsible adult. The overall task thus consists in creating possibilities for these two ends to meet: the objective perspectives and the self-perception and interests of the adults.

Seen from the angle of the objective perspectives, the central issue is whether this is possible, and if so, how we shall be able through education to develop competences and resistancy that are not merely concerned with the acquisition of learning contents, but also with the will and ability to use these in appropriate ways in relevant known and unknown contexts. As described in part 2 of the book, positive results here depend especially on the promotion of the accommodative and possibly transformative processes in all the three dimensions of learning and penetration of parts of the defence and the everyday consciousness that we have all been forced to develop. In practice this involves, at a general level, that *the education programmes must include active acquisition of significant learning contents, the application and testing of what has been learned in relevant situations, and a subsequent processing of the experience and reflection on it. It is also important that this must take place in supportive, open and mutual social and societal contexts.*

Concerning the perspective as seen by the participants, I have formulated the challenge as follows in the concluding report from our research on Danish adult education:

"*The generally most decisive factor for significant learning in adults is the requirement for motivation rooted in direct interest, something they feel like doing and are committed to, or a realised necessity, something they have understood and accepted to be beneficial to learn in relation to something they want to achieve. Furthermore, it is important that the learning situation is of a character that enables adults to 'dare' be open to new impulses, let their defences drop and allow any resistance to be expressed openly.*

If the ideal of lifelong learning is not just to mean lifelong cramming, but is really to be about personal development and broad competences, these prerequisites become more important still. For the more we are concerned with learning that is not merely of intellectual character but includes the entire person with reason, emotions and social reactions, the greater the significance of the motivational and situation-determined context.

In terms of education, these matters mean that if adult education is to have any meaning as something other than storage of unproductive labour, it must be based on and make room for interplay between the learning objectives, the participants' motivational background, prior qualifications and the education situation that is created."
(Illeris 2000, p. 61)

The entirely central element in these formulations is that the work on structuring and executing the education programmes should not, like in traditional didactics and education planning, be perceived as an implementation of the objectives in academic contents and some appropriate work forms, but on the contrary as a question of ways in which the given objectives and the participants in question may be brought to interact with each other, and, let it be noted, based on a realistic and not idealised or moralising perception of the participants. In what follows I shall explore how this might be achieved.

11.2. The significance of division of responsibility

First and foremost, it is of entirely decisive importance that the point of departure of planning is that the participants in adult education programmes are *adults*, humans that both formally and in reality are responsible for their own actions and decisions (cf. section 8.2). At this basic level, I think I am quite in line with Malcolm Knowles in his agitation for "andragogy" as a discipline, which is in many ways different from the pedagogy of children's schooling and upbringing (Knowles 1970, 1973). I disagree, however, with respect to some of the practical consequences, and also find the term "andragogy" too narrow in the same way as "pedagogy" is too narrow to include the societal and organisational aspects of child education.

It is also very important to state that the point of departure mentioned is in line with the basic notions of adult education participants: Our Danish research in adult education clearly implies that the element of adult education programmes which participants react most strongly against is that their responsibility is not respected – perhaps they do not even respect it themselves. To a certain degree this may be because in our school days we all acquired some notions of learning in which precisely the distribution of responsibility is different because the students are children.

The question of division of responsibility is fundamental when we are concerned with adult education, and once we realise this we also receive the key to understanding many apparently irrational matters that make their impact felt in adult education programmes, ranging from general planning to all sorts of small and major practical details at floor-level. This also includes that it is not just the institutions and the teachers who "by default" relate to the participants in a way that imposes a child's role on them by assuming much responsibility which, considered from both an ethical, legal, practical and learning angle, ought to lie with the participants, but that the participants also themselves basically perceive this as natural and legitimate even though they, at the same time, more or less consciously react against it.

Therefore the whole thing is not so simple that we can just decide that adult education within a certain given framework is the participants' responsibility. Those who manage adult education programmes must make an *active* effort not to assume the responsibility, an action which slightly paradoxically also involves that they must accept responsibility for "returning" responsibility to the participants, and this is not as uncomplicated as it may immediately sound. In practice, this has proved to be a highly difficult process, which very often involves surmounting deeply rooted resistance, and it therefore requires perseverance and determination with both teachers and participants (cf. Illeris 1998).

First, for leaders and teachers it is always difficult to surrender their position of power voluntarily and even actively. In addition, *assuming responsibility for not assuming responsibility* appears both paradoxical and contradictory. However, this is precisely what is required, this is the situation in which adult educators very often find themselves, and it is a decisive criterion for a professional adult educator to be able to handle this. Furthermore, the situation may in practice be highly sensitive and emotional, and there is a very fine line between the participants' responsibility for their own learning and education and the teacher's responsibility for providing the optimal conditions for and input to this learning and education; and perhaps even also ultimately to have to assess the results in contexts that may be of crucial importance for the individual participant's future opportunities.

It is, however, of decisive importance that the matters surrounding the division of responsibility is understood and respected at all levels in adult education programmes, because it is the very basis for them to be able to function appropriately, both as concerns learning and economically. As it is today, there is a massive waste of human and economic resources because the widespread ambivalence among participants makes their learning reluctant and ineffective, and creates many problems. Even though many well-qualified and well-meaning teachers, leaders and administrators show great commitment and make exciting experiments and development work, no fundamental change takes place, because the entire system is dyed in a fundamental disempowerment of the participants, which often takes place imperceptibly behind the backs of leaders and teachers and against their best convictions and intentions.

Naturally, this division of responsibility does not mean that the participants can just demand to get public education in whatever strikes their fancy and themselves decide if they can be bothered to turn up or if they can be bothered to do anything, and whatever people who wish to defend the status quo might otherwise imagine. Assuming responsibility means that participants relate to the possibilities offered, make considered choices on this basis and follow up on the choices through action, and possibly protest if something appears unreasonable. Even though many and highly different adults attend adult education programmes, they are generally neither idiots nor opportunists; on the contrary, they are, as a rule, very straightforward and responsible once they realise that they actually have the responsibility.

In the existing system, the participants may easily be perceived as irresponsible just because they hesitate about assuming responsibility for what they ultimately experience that others have decided for them. It may well be that in many cases they would have decided the same thing or something similar themselves, but they have seldom had the opportunity for this because culture dictates that most important decisions are made by others on their behalf. It may also well be that they find it difficult to make decisions themselves when they have the opportunity, but it is after all precisely what development of competence and resistancy to a large extent is meant to produce, and therefore the "system" must not react to such problems by merely assuming responsibility, but on the contrary hold the participants to the fact that it is their responsibility.

What I am calling for is by no means an easy task. First, it is important to structure a system from the ground up so there is a clear and well-reasoned framework to relate to and wide opportunities for the participants themselves to navigate, individually or collectively, within this framework. Second, it is important all the time to be aware of not taking the responsibility which ought to be the participants', also even though they are often, especially at the beginning, inclined to try to avoid the responsibility and try to manoeuvre the teacher back into the usual responsible teacher role. Third, it is important to contribute, in a considered and focused way, to having the participants both take the responsibility for their own learning and understand that this is what they are doing, and that it is important that they do so.

The participants' taking responsibility for their own learning in no way means that there will be less responsibility for the leaders and teachers of the adult education programmes. On the contrary, it may be even more demanding in terms of responsibility when, in the many everyday situations and details, leaders and teachers must constantly decide what may reasonably be considered the participants' own responsibility and what the system and the teacher may and must assume responsibility for, instead of just fulfilling the traditional responsible teacher role that everybody is familiar with from their own school days.

The rest of this book will be dealing with ways in which adult education programmes that endeavour to meet the formulated overall objectives, the participants' needs and interests and the outlined division of responsibility may be structured and put into practice. In the following, I shall explore the general framework, and then there will be chapters dealing with the contents and steering of education programmes, their work forms, learning environment, assessment forms, counselling and guidance. In the fourth and final part of the book, I shall then summarise the main lines of argument in the presented understanding of adult education programmes.

11.3. The frames of adult education

It follows from the above that the most fundamental element when determining the framework for adult education programmes is a point of departure which involves that *none can participate in adult education without having made the positive choice to do so themselves.* Even though many may be insecure and doubting, there must be a decision, and the decision must be the participant's own. Participants may still, of course, receive guidance (which may even be considerably more thorough than is most often the case today, cf. chapter 14), because it is important that the whole framework and all consequences are known. However, the decision must be the participant's own, and it must be a key duty for counsellors, leaders and others to ensure that it really so, so that the extensive waste of resources involved in the education of non-motivated participants can be reduced.

It is also important in relation to the above that the education conditions should not be of a character that amounts to coercion, i.e. that the individual in question is not to be placed in a poorer situation as a consequence of choice of education, economically or otherwise. This is of course a significant political matter, but once one has been out in the broad adult education programmes and observed the number of participants who are there without any real desire on their own part to be there and who have no sense of having chosen to be there themselves, one realises that it is at it both degrading in human and societal terms, and inappropriate in terms of learning.

It is presumably also economically inappropriate when the intended learning more or less fails to materialise, but this is a highly complicated calculation, which I shall not venture into here (the problem is that others actually make such economic calculations, but on a deficient and unacceptable basis, cf. chapter 5).

On the other hand, I do not find that, from a perspective of learning, there is something wrong with a certain level of school fees payable in connection with adult education. On the contrary, our research experience, even though we did not address this issue directly, indicated that the participants generally accept having to pay reasonable school fees, and that it can promote the learning efforts by helping participants take their education more seriously because they have paid to participate. This must, however, be considered in the context of the above, i.e. that direct or indirect coercion must not influence their choice, and in general be understood in the sense that what is "reasonable" must be seen in relation to the participants' economic situation.

Another important matter which came to our awareness through the Adult Didactic Project is the importance of the participants' experience of the activities as thoroughly aimed at and structured for adult participants. It has of course much to do with forms of work and social interaction, elements I shall deal with in chapters 12 and 13, but it is important also in connection with the overall framework.

In addition there are of course many other factors in the framework that are the responsibility of the authorities and which they therefore also must make decisions on. A number of these matters, including e.g. forms of control and assessment I shall consider later, in section 13.7. Other matters are of an administrative character, but may all the same have an impact on learning, like e.g. the size of classes, buildings and classroom facilities, who may teach, the participants' rights and obligations, etc.

These matters may at the same time also have economic and legal implications, and there must of course be a prioritisation of different concerns.

It is important to maintain and expand an adult education system that is broad and varied both as concerns education contents, levels, work forms and geographical location, so that as far as possible courses may be found that offer something subjectively attractive for everybody. Of course there are also societal and commercial interests implicated in this, but if the official definitions of the slogan of lifelong learning and its significance for society and its members are to be taken seriously, we must break away from the favouring of commercial interests that is the current norm.

The narrow commercial orientation is generally shortsighted, and it must also be of commercial interest to foster a more general human and societal development. This obviously does not exclude that adult education programmes must also offer courses that have definite commercial aims, whereas other courses may be solely general in their aim.

11.4. School culture and learning environment

Just as important as the formal framework surrounding the education programmes are the informal matters, the unwritten laws, the tone and spirit that prevail in the programmes, the relations between management, administration, teachers and participants and mutually between people in the individual groups. As a rule, we distinguish between *school* culture, which is concerned with the organisational culture that is found at the individual institution or within certain types of educational institutions, and the *learning environment,* which more directly relates to the conditions and relations that the learning is a direct part of, but we can not make a sharp distinction between the two concepts.

In cooperation with a colleague, I have taken part in analysing the school culture within a number of Danish adult education areas and the cooperation problems between the different school cultures (Andersen & Illeris 1995, cf. section 10.2). We found three highly different types of school cultures, which we termed school oriented (especially in the general adult education programmes), commercially oriented (especially in

the trade oriented adult education programmes) and participant oriented (especially in the day high schools), and we found great problems,
clashes and comprehensibility gaps when different types of school cultures were to co-operate.

Based on the understanding of adult education programmes which
this book is an expression of, especially the school oriented culture is problematic, because it possesses to a special degree the features which
adults experience as forcing them into a child's role, including the relatively tightly structured contents, the traditional class tuition, the subject
orientation, splitting school days into 45-minute portions, grades, attendance records and exams, but also matters like the school-like appearance
and functionality of the buildings, as well as the traditional character of
the lecture rooms. These are factors which indirectly place the participants in the impersonal student role they know all too well from their own
school days, and which they more or less consciously react negatively
against. Both teachers and participants in the general adult education
programmes typically and very often use the phrase, "we ARE adults";
apparently they feel a strong need to make that constantly clear because
they feel very strongly that they are placed in a situation that imposes a
child's status on them.

The commercially oriented school culture is i.a. characterised by the
feel and mood of its institutions having to a much higher degree the character of work places, especially when we consider workshops, and it is
typically perceived as positive, as something that relates to working life
and thereby to adult life. However, there are also negative features, like
e.g. quite a large amount of class tutorials in so-called "theory rooms",
relatively tightly structured contents, tight time schedules and attendance
records. All in all signals that remind the participants of traditional school
attendance and thereby contribute to maintain their ambivalence.

Last, the participant oriented school culture is very conscious of making every effort to ensure that the education programmes function on the
adult participants' terms and prior qualifications, even though there is
also quite a lot of more traditional teaching. The participants often react
to this with surprise, and it can take some time for them to get used to
this unfamiliar culture and its opportunities. However, most of them

eventually perceive it very positively, and may then later start protesting against the features in the culture that still remind them of their school days.

Generally, these images and differences can, to a high degree cause people to notice the elements of the culture that impose a child's role on participants and try to go against them. However, it is not so easy, partly because these elements are entrenched in some well-developed cultural patterns and therefore deeply rooted in the institutions. Such elements also interact with the formal framework conditions and cannot, in many cases, be changed in earnest without also making changes to the formal area.

As concerns the learning environment, the Danish education researcher Bjarne Wahlgren (1999) has described and compared a number of surveys and descriptions from different countries of what can be considered a good learning environment for adult education (C. Rogers 1969, Knowles 1973, Darkenwald 1987, 1989, Scavenius & Wahlgren 1995, A. Rogers 1996). There are many different suggestions, but also recurring features.

One general feature is that the learning environment must be characterised by warmth, care, security, tolerance and emotional attachment. In this connection there is also emphasis on genuineness, respect, frankness, mutual responsibility, openness and listening to each other in the mutual communication. In addition, the teacher is generally expected to provide organisation, leadership, support for the participants and vivid communications. At the same time there is emphasis on the participants' influence and the inclusion of their experiences. In a few of the sources there are also elements like excitement, involvement, freedom, goal orientation, cooperation and a high academic level.

Despite variations between the different contributions, there is a rather high degree of correspondence, which springs from the fact that the sources chosen explicitly take a position of teaching adult self-determining people. The question of responsibility which received special emphasis in the above is only directly considered in one single contribution (Knowles 1973), but this is presumably because that it was only during the 1990s that a number of countries started seeing large numbers of more or less involuntary participants in adult education programmes. If people themselves have chosen to participate, there are rarely problems with responsibility, and it is specifically on this background that the question of responsibility is so important and comes so clearly into focus now.

12. The organisation of adult education programmes

This chapter deals with the general conditions concerning the practical organisation of adult education programmes. Firstly, there is discussion of the fundamental principles of participant direction and problem orientation, which are of central importance when the programmes aim at the development of competences and resistancy. A model is then presented covering the four basic forms of work: teaching, exercises, studies and projects, which are described in more detail on the basis of the type of learning they are aimed at in particular and what it is important to stress. Finally, there is a section dealing with internship as an important supplementary form of learning.

12.1. Participant direction

In connection with the practical structuring of adult education programmes, it is naturally clear that such programmes and courses can be very different with regard to goals, duration, contents, participants' prior qualifications and much more. What they have in common is that the participants are adults, who basically are entitled to be treated as self-directing and responsible, and who in relation to learning function as outlined in chapters 8 and 9. In addition, it must here be maintained that the overall goal-perspective, in accordance with the deliberations in the above, is concerned with development of competence and resistancy, as described in chapter 5.

The core common rationale for structuring of adult education is therefore that the participants themselves have the possibility for and are maintained as directing their learning to the highest possible degree within the given framework. This does not, of course, mean that teachers and others involved cannot and must not plan the courses, but it means partly that this planning must be explained to the participants and be open for changes, partly that the participants are entitled to support and guidance on both the subjects studied and on personal matters for developing their self-direction, and that it must be respected if the participants make different choices than the ones their counsellors, teachers and leaders had in mind.

These matters may naturally appear somewhat sharp when they are drawn up in principle as here, and it is also important that the basic principles are clear to all concerned. However, in daily practice there must be room for all possible flexibility. The principles are precisely concerned with the foundations that are necessary for genuine and focused cooperation and for creating space for equality and dialogue.

Naturally there are leaders and teachers, because they are able to contribute something that the participants need, so the interplay can never be symmetrical. On the contrary, it is important to acknowledge the different roles and functions. It is the responsibility and function of leaders and teachers to lay down the general framework and provide relevant subject input, good working conditions, necessary tools and generally support and help the participants as well as possible in their learning processes. The participants are responsible for completing the learning in accordance with their possibilities and needs, taking responsibility for this and in connection with this also protest if the activities do not seem appropriate to them. It is this interplay which, way back in 1974, I termed *participant direction*, i.e. joint steering of the learning process as the key factor, and with an obligation for both parties to protest if they do not perceive the learning activities as reasonable (cf. e.g. Illeris 1999).

For many reasons it is very important to maintain the entirely fundamental place of participant direction in adult education programmes and not to confuse it with self-direction, which is either a general feature of adult learning (cf. chapter 8), or a form of organisational design in which the teacher takes no responsibility and acts only when asked to do so by the learner.

First, as mentioned above, participant direction is what adults may justifiably expect in a democratic society, and conversely what a democratic society may justifiably expect its members to engage in. The requirement for participant direction in adult education programmes is

basically an ethical matter, and basically it is, equally, lacking or insufficient participant direction that underlies many adults' experience of
being disempowered and made to play a child's role when they "are sent
back to school".

Second, participant direction is of decisive importance for participants to meet overall goal perspectives on competence and resistancy as
these concepts have been defined previously in this book. When the education programmes generally must reach beyond the acquisition of the
content of a subject and into areas of personality, a factor inherent to the
concepts of competence resistancy, it means of necessity that the participants must involve themselves personally. This presupposes that one has
influence, that one takes part in deciding what is to take place and is not
merely cast in the role of recipient.

Third, and in extension of this, participant direction is also necessary
for learning. If the learning is to reach beyond the assimilative level and
more or less random accommodations, it requires a personal motivation
that is able to mobilise the psychological energy that focused accommodative and perhaps transformative learning processes require.

It has already previously been discussed that even though participant
direction so clearly is in the participants' interest and in a decisive way
increases the possibilities that significant learning can take place, many
participants in adult education programmes do not immediately find this
acceptable and are not spontaneously willing to play an active role. There
are usually good reasons for this, and it is perhaps the most important
explanation of why participant direction is not very extensive in most
adult education programmes today. Nonetheless, this is such a decisive
matter that it becomes the teachers' key task to establish serious and thorough participant direction, in particular often at the start of a course.

12.2. Problem orientation

The other key matter in connection with the structuring of adult education programmes is concerned with the nature of the content, i.e. what
the participants work with and learn from.

It is common that the contents of the education programmes are determined in the shape of a curriculum covering a specific academic field, possibly supplemented with specified indications of level. The curriculum concept is thus closely associated with traditional methods, i.e. that education programmes are structured on the basis of certain specific subjects and disciplines that together cover and define what must be learned.

In some contexts where the aim is solely to acquire a certain subject material such a curriculum framework may perhaps be appropriate. However, generally this is not how the world is structured for the participants in adult education. On the contrary, they structure their environment in *thematic areas* and *problem fields*. In any case that is not concerned with largely school and education oriented material, these are the kinds of structures or categories in terms of which adults think and act.

The difference between on the one hand subjects and curriculum and on the other hand themes and problems, is fundamentally this where subject and curriculum are areas constructed in advance, information for the individual is prior and externally given and content-determined. Themes and problem fields, however, are more fluid areas that constantly develop and change form and are subjectively filled in by the individual based on his/her personal interplay with the surroundings.

If there are no very special reasons, curriculum provisions should therefore be avoided as overall content frames in adult education programmes. They have a tendency to create an approach to the education work that is fundamentally alienating, and they are therefore ultimately a type of exercise of power that should not be applied to adults in a democratic society. This contributes to generating a stronger experience in the participants being disempowered and treated like children.

It is, quite possible to define the necessary content framework in terms of thematic areas and problem fields described in broad and open formulations. Then the participants' subjective perceptions are able become part of and influence what the course is actually concerned with in terms of content in an entirely different way. These areas and problem fields will probably to a considerable extent cover the same matters as those that would have been chosen for an up-to-date curriculum. It is worth noting that curriculum provisions have a persistent tendency not to be quite current, to lag a little behind, perhaps because the tradition of the subjects is also the power base of those who define the curriculum. The same content can assume an entirely different character when it has been selected on the basis of the participants' experience, problems, perspectives on the future, and formulations than when it has been determined in formal executive orders and teaching plans.

In addition it may be said that while the work with a curriculum is fundamentally concerned with the acquisition of specific information on a given subject, the work with themes fundamentally assumes the character of enlightening, and when considering problems the work will produce both enlightenment and possible attempts at solutions. With this in focus, there will be far better possibilities that matters of the subject may be treated on the basis of such a combination of academic, personal and societal angles. This to a far higher degree than a narrower subject-focused approach is able to contribute to the development of competences and resistancy, and in connection with this overview, environment-orientation, competence to choose and act, reflection, reflexivity, critical thinking, self-containment, cooperation, collectivity and social responsibility (cf. chapter 5). All this simply because the subjective and social factors are allotted another place and legitimacy in the courses. Problem orientation is of key significance, not least when we consider the development of resistancy, because it is precisely in connection with discovering and working through problems that there is basis for getting glimpses of matters that require critical review and finding other ways to react (Illeris 1999).

I have chosen here to use both the terms "thematic areas" and "problem fields" because it may be easier to describe academic content as thematic areas. Yet it is important learning-wise to assume a *problem oriented* approach as best promoting the creation of a direct connection between the individual's own subjective perception angle and the content field being considered.

It is first and foremost when one works with finding out where the important problems lie, when one tries to formulate problems with precision and to develop patterns of understanding and proposals for solutions that the full learning challenge is established. Therefore problem orientation in the area of content is ultimately the most consistent concept to base the work on, i.e. what implies the strongest encouragement to work with the learning content in ways that lead to the deep and coherent understanding and the emotional and social involvement through which competence and resistancy development are established (cf. Illeris 1974 p. 78ff, 1981 p. 97ff).

12.3. Forms of work

I have now presented participant direction and problem orientation as the two fundamental concepts for the structuring of adult education programmes. This implies that I consider the questions of *direction* and *selection of content* to be the two most decisive educational dimensions, i.e. the two dimensions that have the most vital importance for the relationship between course structuring and learning.

Based on these dimensions, a model can be constructed to explain different fundamental working approaches in education programmes and the types of learning or knowledge which they are especially suited for developing. Figure 5 shows a model which I have developed on the basis of David Kolb's model for experiential learning (Kolb 1984, Illeris 1995. p. 131ff) (see next page).

In the model, *direction* and *content* have been placed as the two central axes with which the structuring of education courses are concerned. Direction is the vertical axis extending between the poles of *teacher direction* and *participant direction*. Teacher direction has been chosen as a comprehensive term for everything directed by representatives of the education system, including also all legal authorities, school boards, institution management, and ultimately the teachers who act as the system's direct representatives vis-à-vis the participants. Participant direction is the term for the share in direction exercised by the participants in the education programmes (including also the teachers to the extent they personally contribute to direction within the given framework in direct interplay with the other participants).

The horizontal axis is concerned with the selection and character of the contents, and it extends between curriculum or *subject orientation* and

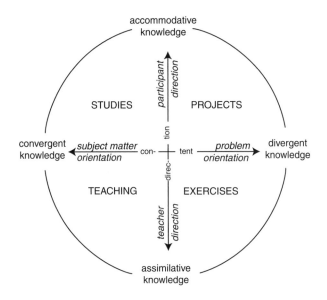

Figure 5: A didactic model.

problem orientation. Subject orientation means that pre-selected academic content determines which activities education programmes are based on, while problem orientation means that thematic areas and/or problem fields are posed, and the participants' problem-focusing approach to this provides the basis for activities.

In terms of learning, the poles of the two axes point towards the form of learning or knowledge that is typically promoted in extension of the weighting of these poles. Teacher direction promotes *assimilative knowledge,* subject matter orientation promotes *convergent knowledge*, subject matter direction promotes *accommodative knowledge*, and problem orientation promotes *divergent knowledge*.

The concepts of assimilative and accommodative have already been described in detail in 6.2. They designate learning in which new knowledge is added to previous knowledge without restructuring, and learning in which the encounter between the new and the previous knowledge produces a restructuring and thereby a qualitative transgression of the previous knowledge.

The concepts of convergent and divergent knowledge were originally developed by the American psychologist and intelligence researcher, John Guilford (1967), and have since been used by David Kolb (1984) in his construction of the model of experiential learning. Convergent knowledge designates a form of perception that centres on one specific explanation of a matter, a specific output from a given input, i.e. typically what we call inferences or deduction. Conversely, divergent knowledge designates a form of understanding in which there may be several valid explanations of a matter, several outputs from a given input, or a form of versatility or diversity thinking, probably of a more creative character.

The four result fields between the axes of the model in figure 5 then show four typical educational work approaches dictated by the chosen forms of direction and content selection and that promote (but do not determine) certain forms of knowledge:

1. A combination of teacher direction and subject orientation means *teaching* in its commonly known form, and it promotes especially assimilative and convergent knowledge.
2. A combination of teacher direction and problem orientation means *exercises* imposed by the teacher or other authorities that may range from simple calculations to large complicated assignments. This promotes especially assimilative and divergent knowledge.
3. A combination of participant direction and subject orientation means *studies*, i.e. that the participants themselves work on acquiring a given material, which promotes accommodative and convergent knowledge.
4. A combination of participant direction and problem orientation means *projects*, where it is the participants' own problem that provide the basis for elucidation, processing and possibly solution proposals. This approach promotes accommodative and divergent knowledge.

The point of this model is not generally to emphasise specific educational approaches, but on the contrary to point out that different fundamental educational approaches have certain characteristics which have an impact on the character of the knowledge or learning that takes place. The educational structuring must therefore be selected and weighed on the basis of reflections on the purpose of the education programme in question. As a rule, at least for all but the very short courses, the choice will/ought to be a combination of two or more types of approach, but in a well-considered balance that corresponds to the purpose of the courses in question (cf. van der Veen 2003).

If the purpose involves development of competence and resistancy, as has been assumed at a general level in the above, it will, as a rule, be appropriate that projects are included with significant weight. If one agrees with the opinion of this book, i.e. that development of competences and resistancy should have a significant position in most adult education programmes, it must therefore also generally mean that projects are accorded a correspondingly significant position. However, the courses may also be relatively short and very focused on practical concerns, which e.g. typically aim to train a specific set of skills within IT, welding, foreign language training, etc., and in such cases it may be reasonable that the main emphasis is placed on teaching and exercises.

In what follows, I shall take a closer look at each of these four forms of work and look at their place, character and possibilities in connection with adult education. Teaching, exercises and studies are considered in each of the three following sections, while projects will be more thoroughly considered in the next chapter, because this work form is less known and developed outside the Scandinavian countries.

Last in this chapter there will be a section on internship, which lies outside the school based work forms, but may be combined with them all, and in many ways add a dimension of very important significance.

12.4. Teaching

Traditional teacher-directed and subject-oriented teaching is in a number of different variations in adult education like most other education programmes by far the commonest form of activity. Under certain conditions, it is also a fine and appropriate framework for essential learning processes in the participants, but it is a serious problem that this work form is also used to a great extent without these conditions being met. Therefore it is important to take a closer look at these conditions.

The first condition is that what must be learned is suited for learning by means of teaching. Teaching may be a good form for mediating certain subject material which the participants need to acquire, and it is therefore also very logical that teaching has been the dominant work form in a school where acquisition of subject material has been perceived to be the predominant aim of the education. However, in modern adult education, where the aims are concerned with the development of competences and similar, teaching is not of necessity an appropriate form of activity, and if it is used more or less automatically, perhaps because habit and tradition dictate that education and teaching are synonymous, the form may well obstruct achievement of the aims because they fundamentally involve a subordination of the participants in relation to the teacher and the material, a subordination that may promote inability to think and act independently, irresponsibility, passivity and distance in relation to the area of applicability.

The other condition is that the participants must be motivated for acquiring the subject content concerned. In some cases, such motivation may be present immediately, e.g. because the participants have signed up for the course in question precisely with a view to acquiring the subject. In such case, it will, as a rule, be sufficient for the teacher to explain and argue for the teaching on the basis of the aim of the course. In other cases, the motivation may arise when the participants in their daily lives or through other education activities experience that they need the basis provided by a certain subject, e.g. specific knowledge, certain skills, insight into the structure of different matters, or how they have been perceived or discussed among key persons or certain schools of thought.

When the participants are motivated for acquiring a certain subject, it may thus be appropriate that this subject is presented in the form of teaching, possibly in interplay with other activity forms. In some cases, there may even be sense in using rather traditional or "informing" teaching, e.g. for a short, focused course in a certain material which the participants have realised that they need to acquire, or if, in connection with a project or similar, such needs arise. In such contexts there is nothing disempowering for adults in working with narrow focus on realising this acquisition as quickly as possible.

However, in most cases by far where the conditions for using teaching as a work form in adult education is present, it will be appropriate to use broader and more dialogue-oriented approaches. The point is first and foremost to use teaching as a basis for creating coherence between the participants' prior qualifications and understanding in the area and the new material to be acquired. "Informing" teaching in principle leads exclusively to assimilative learning, and accommodations are rare and only random occurrences. However, creating a dialogue on the academic content increases the possibilities for accommodative transgressions. In practice, the point is to make connections to the way in which the material in question forms part of the participants' academic, personal and social situation in the broadest sense, i.e. to address questions like what this means to the participants in their everyday lives, their work lives and for the society they are part of, from the local to the global level.

I shall not go into more detail with this. There are many books that provide detailed consideration of approaches for teaching of adults, in which teaching is normally also related to other work forms (e.g. Cooper & McIntyre 1996, Corder 2002). The concern here has been to demonstrate what teaching as an educational work form may be used for and not used for in adult education programmes.

12.5. Exercises

Exercises are also a classical work form in education programmes, most often as a supplement to teaching, e.g. typically in the form of calculations, essays in own and foreign languages, practical exercises in workshop skills training and, gradually, also as a common element in most subjects.

Exercises may naturally be a fine variation element in relation to ordinary teaching, and with the clear advantage that they involve a high degree of participant activity. However, exercises are also, when they are given and defined by the teacher, fundamentally a subordinating work form, in which the participants must do what others have decided. They can, in their common form, to a certain degree contribute to a development of competence, but have rarely any significance for the development of resistancy.

However, the term "exercise" as a work form, as it has been defined here, has very wide reference, and some important elements may enter the picture if the exercises are collective efforts, as typically in different forms of group work, or major, complicated exercises that require independent structuring of a multi-faceted work process. The more the exercises move in this direction, the greater importance they may have for up-to date competence development, even though the form is in principle limited by the general teacher direction.

In this connection, it is important to mention the work form that has been termed problem-based learning (PBL), and which through the last 20 years has gained considerable currency, especially in medical studies, but also in other primarily natural science and technical education programmes, e.g. in Sweden (University of Linköping) and the Netherlands (University of Maastricht), where the form has been developed very thoroughly and systematically.

The tasks here considered are extensive and at the same time very goal-oriented, which precisely in connection with competence development may be highly appropriate, not least in the areas mentioned, but perhaps also to a certain extent in other areas to which certain very central and unavoidable problem fields are integral. At the same time it is important to be aware of the limitation of independence involved in the fact that exercises are assigned from outside. It is hardly appropriate if the entire course of the education fails to include participant determined projects in which the problems that the participants themselves experience in relation to the field of the education may be considered.

12.6. Studies

Studies are first and foremost the classical work form for university students, but in recent decades the form has gained wider currency, not least in the forms known as open studies and distance studies. This also involves extensive use of ICT, but it is characteristic that the use of this gives the highest significance when the point is precisely to transcend the classic study form and to a higher degree involve current communication with others, cf. 10.5.

Studies possess some obvious practical advantages. They are not, or only to a limited extent, tied to an education situation with regard to time and place, and participants can therefore plan studies freely on the basis of their possibilities and needs. They also offer the participants great freedom with respect to their position on the academic content, which, admittedly, in principle is defined in advance and from outside.

However, studies are also as a point of departure a lonely work form, in which the exchange with others is limited to a few meetings and indirect communication. However, it is precisely this side of the work form which has been increasingly adjusted in the open education programmes and distance learning, and it has turned out that for participants with sufficient motivation and self-discipline, studies under these forms may at once profit by the great degrees of freedom and at the same time have a considerable social attachment which at least to a certain degree can contribute to realisation of the development of competences and resistancy. However, if the necessary motivation and self-discipline are not there, the work form involves a very great risk of dropout and/or limitations to learning.

12.7. Internships

As far back as the Middle Ages, practical training has been the central element in apprenticeship. Over time, more and more school education has been added; however, internships remain crucially important, not least if the apprentices are consulted, and the "workshop practical training" which schools have had to introduce because there are not enough trainee positions available do not provide the same learning experience.

Internship is also a significant element in the so-called profession education programmes, i.e. the medium-cycle further education programmes qualifying teachers, educators, nurses, social workers, etc. The adult education programmes proper have not, however, usually included a trainee element in the same way.

Seen from the perspective of development of competence and resistancy assumed in this book, there is every reason to take an interest in internship as an educational activity that can form part of alternation with the school-based activities. It is, after all, in confrontation with practice that vocational qualifications can be developed into competences. However, it does not just happen. Quite the contrary, it has through the entire history of the practical training education programmes been a central problem to create the coherence between school learning and internship supposed to result in the desired competence development. Thus, it is not coincidental that, parallel with the interest in the concept of competence, there has been increasing interest in internship , which has been posed as a counter-model to "scholastic" learning in the educational institutions (e.g. Wackerhausen 1997).

With regard to the perception of learning, recent decades have seen the development of two important main currents in practice learning. One has centred on the concepts of "situated learning" and "communities of practice" as they have especially been developed in the USA by Jean Lave and Etienne Wenger (Lave & Wenger 1991, Wenger 1998, cf. chapter 10), which has led to an interest in the "rehabilitation of apprenticeship", i.e. of apprenticeship-like arrangements for a broad range of different education programmes (Journal of Nordic Educational Research 1997). The other has taken an interest in what characterises the learning courses that make some people "experts" or "reflective practitioners", (Dreyfus & Dreyfus 1986, Schön 1983, 1987), and it has to a higher degree led to an interest for learning directly in working life (e.g. Billett 2001).

The main impression is, as already mentioned in chapter 10, that on the one hand there are great possibilities for development of both competence and resistancy associated with learning courses in working life, but that, on the other hand, it does not just happen automatically. It requires planned and supported interplay with courses that take place with a certain distance to the work and provides the possibility for processing and reflecting on experience and connecting it with theory and further personal and societal related perspective-building (Illeris 2003c).

There is thus every reason to take an interest in ways in which different adult education programmes may include internships. However, it is important in this connection to develop interplay so what is acquired in a school course is used and tested in practice, and experience from practical training is made the object of discussion and reflection in school programmes. It is also vitally important that resources are made available in the form of paid time for the teachers and counsellors involved, to allow them to plan and ensure that such interplay is actually established.

13. Project work in adult education

In this short chapter – which was especially written for the English edition of this book – the principles, practice and some relevant challenges of project work as an educational method are briefly outlined and commented on. It is emphasised that for more than thirty years there has been a great deal of experience with this kind of practice on all educational levels in the Scandinavian countries. At the same time, it is stressed that although some fundamental principles and a series of typical phases have been identified, the best way of learning how to practise and supervise project work is simply to try it out and reflect individually and collectively on the process, experience and problems that emerge.

13.1. Project studies

In the previous chapter 'project' was identified as the term for educational activities which are fundamentally structured by the principles of participant direction and problem orientation. This term can be traced back to the American educator William Kilpatrick who, in his efforts to transform John Dewey's educational thoughts into practical directions, worked out the so-called project method (Kilpatrick 1918, Dewey 1934). However, this was a method for individual studies, whereas the educational practice of project work which has been under development since the 1970s, mainly in the Scandinavian countries and Germany, and is widely practised in the public educational systems in Denmark and Norway, was generated mainly as a procedure for group work with a theoretical basis in pedagogical principles related to contemporary educational demands (Illeris 1999, Nielsen & Webb 1999, Schäfer 1988).

The fundamental principles of *participant direction* and *problem orientation* have already been explained in parts 12.1. and 12.2. But three other important principles are also implied in the foundation of project work.

The principle of *exemplarity* implies that the problems and content material chosen for a project should be a representative example of a larger and essential area of reality. Through deep and serious work on a genuine problem of personal and general interest, the underlying structures of the problem area are to be uncovered in order to enable the students to generalise their insight into new contexts.

The principle of *interdisciplinarity implies* that the chosen problem forms the basis for the choice of content, theories and methods that are taken up independent of the academic or professional subjects or disciplines in which they originate, and that it is only under special conditions that a problem which is closely related to a specific subject or discipline should be accepted.

The principle of *group work* implies that projects should normally be carried out in groups, thereby not only taking advantage of the wider range of input, perspectives and opinions and the larger working capacity of the group, but also involving practical training in cooperation, division of labour, coordination and collective work procedures in general, as these skills constitute an important part of qualification for today's society and labour market.

Thus project work is seen as the practical organisation of education that, in general, most adequately meets both the late modern demands for competence development and the need for such individual and collective training as can enhance the elements of resistancy as described in chapter 5.

13.2. The practice of project work

Educational projects may have duration of anything between a few hours and several years according to the type and length of the education of which they are a part. However, it is important to realise and respect the fact that they are *educational* projects that differ fundamentally from professional or private projects in that their basic objective is the learning and competence development of the participants. Of course, the project's results may also be important, but this can be regarded as a welcome secondary effect which may actually also make a major contribution to the learning outcome, as the results created by the participants themselves will be of great personal significance and importance.

The course of a typical project can, no matter its total duration, be broken down into a typical series of phases. But it must be understood that this implies an analytical reduction, that not all phases need to occur in all projects, that the order may be changed, and that it is possible to be in two or more phases at the same time or to return to past phases. With these reservations the following eight phases can be distinguished.

1. *Introduction.* The extent and nature of the introductory phase is dependent on whether or not the participants are already acquainted with this approach. In all cases there must be an introduction to the time and content frames of the projects and other regulations and practical conditions that must be respected, and this must be clear to participants by the end of the phase. There should also always be some kind of introduction to the subject area in question, and this should not just take the form of a statement or an account, but be organised in an appealing, provocative and activating way to cause ideas and problems to be actualised and developed in the students as a platform for the following phases. If all participants do not already have personal experience of project work, there should also be an introduction to the principles and practice of the method. However, this should not be too elaborate, as it seems to be very difficult for students to imagine what it is all about before the various issues arise in practice. Finally, a thorough social introduction of the participants to each other is very important if they do not all know each other in advance. Sometimes these various functions can be united in a pilot project, which is a brief, well-guided and well-prepared project that should be able to raise more problems than it resolves.

2. *The choice of theme.* The actual project course commences with a phase that usually simultaneously includes a choice of project theme inside the given content or problem area, and the formation of project groups and allocation of supervisors. The theme should be chosen in accordance with the principle of exemplarity so that it involves both

the engagement of the students and a relevant content area. Groups are usually formed on the basis of interest in content matter, and supervisors are also allocated on this basis, although they need not necessarily be experts on the themes to which they are allocated. It is also important to realise and accept that social preferences and aversions play an important role in the group formation process.

3. *Problem formulation.* In this phase the project group should precisely formulate the specific problems that the project is to deal with. This formulation has proved to be a very important process, because not only does it create the starting point of the project, it is also a process which, if taken seriously, will uncover a lot of bias, opinions, expectations, inclinations and interests of the different group members and thereby force the group to make a series of fundamental decisions. Problem formulation is a very significant issue in the project method, and it is important that both students and supervisor pay the utmost attention to all details in the formulation so that it can function as a common statement of precisely what the group has agreed on.

4. *Practical planning.* After the problem formulation, it is time for a phase that includes planning of time, delegation of tasks, internal and external appointments, process evaluation, etc. The supervisor will usually be useful in this phase to render assistance in the choice of relevant literature or other input and to establish contacts in the practice area chosen if the group members do not already have such contacts. It is also important to agree on a division of labour which is both fair and respects the different individual interests and potentialities of the group members, and to prepare for a work process which ensures that the different contributions can be adjusted and combined to form a joint whole and not just a collection of more or less independent and isolated parts.

5. *The investigation phase.* Now comes the long and central phase of the project in which, in order to probe the problem area selected, an attempt is made to establish an ever-increasing understanding, to re-

late it to relevant theory, etc. In this phase it is especially important to have a high degree of internal coordination, to write down all agreements, decisions, references, extracts of relevant literature, ideas, drafts, etc. Another important feature is the communication between the project group and the supervisor, who must find the difficult balance of providing professional guidance without forcing the group to accept his or her own interests or points of view.

6. *The product phase.* In this phase a written report and/or other products such as illustrations, tapes, meetings, performances or the like are produced. This is important not only in relation to assessment and exams, but also because the production of such products in forms that can be comprehended by others, forces the group to genuinely complete the project. In order to make the report or other product, the project participants must formulate or in other ways communicate their results and therefore also agree on them and express them in precise terms. This normally implies that all participants really come to realise and understand what they have learned in relation to the content of the project. Very often in this phase, time will be short, and the group must therefore find out how to dispose, coordinate and produce the product in the most expedient and effective way, which is often a hard but also very useful learning process.

7. *Product evaluation.* The evaluation of the product may be an internal assessment by other students and supervisors, but in most cases it is a formal external examination. However, this examination is quite different from the usual kind of inquiry, because its starting point is the report or other product of the students and not a randomly chosen topic inside the curriculum. It usually takes the form of a group examination with individual grading to ensure that all members of the project group are active in the process. (Most often all participants receive the same grade, but there are also many examples where differentiation has been found necessary by the examiners, who are usually the supervisor and an external professional).

8. *Post-evaluation.* When the formal evaluation has taken place the project is usually regarded as completed. However, in most cases it is a good idea to add a short extra phase in which the group is gathered, if possible with their supervisor, and where each member makes a final internal statement of the benefits and consequences of the project and these statements are discussed. It may be a session of one or two hours, perhaps finishing with some kind of celebration if the project has been of a considerable duration and importance for the participants. Although this phase is optional and lies after the official termination of the project, it can comprise a most valuable contribution to the learning process because it forces each group member, as well as the group collectively, to reflect on the process and the learning it has entailed.

As already mentioned, this description of the project phases should not be regarded as a prescription but rather as a survey for inspiration and support. The crucial features of the project process are the problem formulation at the outset and the making of a manifest product as a conclusion.

The problem formulation is important for several reasons. It forces the project group to really agree in detail on what the project is to be about. It also serves as a basis for the direction of the project and the common statement to be referred to in case of doubt or disagreement later on. And as many projects are actually changed along the way when new aspects are discovered or new understandings develop, a corresponding change of the problem formulation will make clear and visible the idea of the change and why it is found necessary. Finally, the problem formulation is again a valuable basis for the final evaluation as well as a possible post-evaluation, helping participants and evaluators to see what was intended and what the outcome has been.

The production of a manifest product is important because it forces the project group and its participants to clarify the results of the project and thereby also to work out their reasons and arguments in ways that enable others to comment and evaluate the process as well as the product.

In between these two requirements, the central content work is accomplished and has its own meaning and motivation – and this is why the participation in and commitment of all participants to decisions in these phases are so important. The project must be experienced as the students' own endeavour and responsibility and not just a requirement set up by others in order to fulfil the personal sort of learning involving development of competence and resistancy.

Finally, it is also important to mention that the first four phases, which deal with preparing and establishing a basis for the investigation, are equally important and necessary for the process, and, at least for beginners, may very well take one third or even half of the project time – which is often a problem for an inexperienced and impatient supervisor. But in project work, a considerable part of the transcending learning processes takes place in the phases where the group finds out what to investigate together, how to do it, and why.

13.3. Some important challenges

The concept of project work as outlined above was first worked out in detail in the early years of Roskilde University, which was established in 1972 to relieve and constitute an alternative to the more traditional university in Copenhagen. From here it has spread to other parts of the Danish education system, to the other Scandinavian countries and, to a limited extent, to other countries also, where it has often been combined with similar, but often less radical, concepts and ideas. Today it has, as already mentioned, a solid and acknowledged position in the Scandinavian countries and is, for instance, part of the curriculum in primary and secondary school and in many parts of youth and adult education in Denmark and Norway. Of course, the outlines have been adjusted to the various educational fields where it has been introduced, but in general the basic principles have been maintained.

However, during all these years opposition to both the ideas and the practice of project education has been strong, especially from traditional academic positions and from right-wing political forces and the educational back-to-basics movement. In these circles, the project concept has always been regarded with suspicion, and the sceptical question has been repeated again and again: Do the students really learn what they are supposed to?

Behind the question is obviously a quantitative idea of learning related to the ability to reproduce the contents of a fixed syllabus. In the first place, therefore, it must be emphasised that when project work was introduced, it was precisely in opposition to this idea of what learning should be. Already then, more than thirty years ago, this idea had proved inadequate in relation to the qualification demands of contemporary society, and in the meantime general societal development, including the ideas of lifelong learning and development of competence, has certainly involved a growing need for less traditional conceptions of learning and education.

But it must also be stressed that the contrast between project work and traditional teaching does not come down to a question of either/or. As already stated in the previous chapter, only in very few and specific cases should an educational course be totally dominated by one single way of working. In the case of project work, a balance must also always be found between projects and more traditional study activities such as teaching, lectures, exercises and individual studies.

Another important question has to do with students' attitudes and consciousness. When the concept of project work was introduced in the 1970s it seemed quite easy for the students to find suitable problems that met the fundamental requirement of representing an objective problem, i.e. existing and having significance in the real world, and be subjective or personal, thus engaging the student and providing the drive and motivation to cope with it and, hopefully, to solve it. It was usually not difficult to formulate such problems. There was a multitude of them, and important societal problems were very often also regarded and experienced as personal problems.

To some extent this seems to have changed, and personal experience has come increasingly into focus. Younger students of today, in particular, tend to be more personal in their interests, and this is a very important source of motivation, creativity, and authenticity in projects. But it sometimes also implies that it is difficult for such students to explain the general significance of the problems with which they choose to deal.

When this is the case, the principle of exemplarity is invalidated. The problem chosen does not function psychologically as an example of a field of reality and, therefore, what is learned is more or less limited to the example itself and cannot be generalised into a broader area. Therefore, during the last decade or more many discussions about project work have concentrated on the principle of exemplarity, the importance of its maintenance, how it may be differentiated to serve more precisely in relation to different fields of education, and how its application in practice can be ensured without limiting reasonable student influence (e.g. Christiansen 1999).

Finally, I would like to mention an important issue in this connection: the training of teachers to serve adequately as project supervisors. In the early years, no teachers were trained or very well equipped for this task, and we all had to plunge into the challenge and find our way to a practice that functioned. In the intervening years many efforts have been initiated to solve this problem, and as I see it there is a general conclusion which is quite clear: the best way to learn to supervise projects is through carrying out projects and analysing and reflecting individually and collectively on all the aspects and problems that emerge. However, active and concentrated courses in which typical problems and conflicts in project work are played through and discussed or where the participants try to supervise in brief, constructed situations which are recorded on video and replayed for discussion, can also be very effective for teachers who already have some experience as supervisors.

Of course, it is also a good idea that supervisors as well as students study the concept and theory of project work. However, the general experience is that if this is done in advance, when there is no personal experience to which to relate the theories and instructions, it becomes much too abstract to have any significant practical value.

14. The implementation of adult education

In this chapter the practical implementation of adult education programmes is taken up, not the many major or minor practical details but a number of more general practical matters. At first there is a discussion of the teachers' functions, where it is emphasised that today the necessary professional and pedagogical competence must be linked to professionalism and authenticity. Then a number of other important areas are discussed which are of importance for the programmes' quality, nature, and possibility of living up to objectives concerning the development of competences and resistancy: the division of responsibility, security and challenges, activity, collectivity, and individuality, reflection and reflexivity. Finally the very important issues concerning control and evaluation are dealt with.

14.1. The teacher in adult education

In the practical execution of adult education courses it is vital that teachers work directly together with the participants and thereby exercise the practical institutional responsibility. It is therefore natural to begin with a discussion of the "teacher role" in adult education programmes.

I place the word "teacher role" inside quotation marks because the most important thing in this connection is, in my opinion, that there is no definite role which is the right one and which an teacher in an adult education programme must try to fill. On the contrary, adult participants today greatly emphasise their preference that the teachers are "authentic", i.e. themselves, and also experience and relate to the participants as they are. So if there exists such a thing as a teacher role for the adult teacher, it is this double authenticity we should be concerned with. It is characterised precisely by being not a role in the traditional sense, something given which the teacher is to step into, but on the contrary an expression of who the teacher actually is and how the teacher may relate to others as they are.

Instead of exploring an imaginary teacher role, I thus find it much more appropriate to focus on ways in which the teacher, in interplay with the participants, may develop and constantly develop further as a teacher who, on the basis of academic and personal competences, can support the participants in the adult education programmes in their own development of competences and resistancy in an appropriate manner. In this perspective it becomes important all the time to be aware of one's functions and one's interplay with the participants, that one notices how it functions and what might function better, or, to use a modern expression, that one maintains a reflexive attitude to one's job. This is also the core point of the many discussions and initiatives on teacher professionalism, teacher authenticity, etc., which have played an increasing role since the beginning of the 1990s (e.g. Brookfield 1990, Wildemeersch 2000).

Where the teacher was earlier first and foremost perceived as a mediator of academic contents who was in particular to "master the subject" and then be able to communicate the subject to the participant group in question, we are today also concerned with being able to facilitate or support the participants' learning and being a good guide and role model for the participants. This involves both an academic identity that relates to the contents of a subject area and a pedagogical identity that relates to the interplay with the participants and to a great extent also an ego-identity or self-identity (Giddens 1991) relating to the teacher's relation to him or herself as a teacher.

These greatly expanded demands on teachers, not least within adult education programmes, are closely connected with the fact that the development of competences is something more than and different from the development of academic qualifications. The personal and social dimensions are inherent in the competences and thereby in what must be learned. In addition, with resistancy as a further perspective it is made clear that the participants' development must constantly be understood in a dialectic perspective, that we are concerned with a duality which both involves necessary competences and the ability and will to assume a reflective attitude to these competences and understand them in a broader context than the directly academic context. It is not least the teacher's way of functioning in the interplay between the content-related and the personal elements that is of vital importance for whether or not the competence development also comes to include resistancy.

What was once referred to as the "teacher role" has, in the same way as the challenge posed to participants in adult education programmes, developed into becoming a matter that ranges across a wide spectrum, from job-related qualifications to the teacher's way of administering her or his personality on the job. In the following sections, this will form part of discussions of different aspects in connection with the practice of adult education programmes.

14.2. Division of responsibility in practice

As already described in section 11.2., the question of division of responsibility, especially between teachers and participants, is probably the most central issue that constitutes the material difference between adult education and other school attendance. While the participants must of necessity have and accept responsibility for their own learning, the responsibility for a carefully considered and appropriate academic input and for creating the best possible conditions for education rests with teachers, and here lies also the responsibility for addressing and handling the question of division of responsibility (cf. Illeris 1998). This may in practice be done in many different ways, which in principle may be placed along a continuum between what I shall call the direct and the gradual approach.

When using the direct approach, the teacher addresses the issue immediately. At the beginning of an educational course, the question of division of responsibility is raised as one of the first items, and the teacher or teachers make it clear that the participants themselves must assume responsibility for their learning, while it is the teacher's responsibility to support them in their efforts and provide the best possibilities conditions for them. This must of course be substantiated, both in principle and in relation to learning, and it must be explained how this can function in practice, including when and how the teachers are available. It is also important to be aware that this approach is unsuitable if there are a large number of participants who in advance are sceptical about the course and feel more or less forced to participate.

The consistent direct approach causes the outlined division of responsibility to take effect immediately. Teachers e.g. tell that they consider fundamental academic material at certain times when the participants have the opportunity to be present, and that generally books, material and workshops are available within specified times when they themselves are available for counselling, and which demands and guidelines that generally apply. It is important for the participants to be able to administer their responsibility that there is complete openness and clarity concerning the framework.

Subsequently, the responsibility is actually handed over to the participants. Experience shows that this causes the participants to feel that they are in a sort of vacuum, which can be very frustrating and often finds expression in a strongly aggressive attitude towards the teachers: "What do you really think they're paying you for, anyway?" If teachers wish to follow this approach, they must therefore be prepared for this phase and for reacting with kindness and understanding, but at the same time without wavering maintain the division of responsibility that has been introduced.

The phase may well last for several days, in some cases for a week or more, but if the teachers can maintain their position and stick to their arguments, the participants will eventually try to get going and ask the teachers for support for their efforts. When they really realise that they themselves are running the show and that they can actually utilise the teachers' time and the other facilities, a number of activities gradually get going, and an almost euphoric mood can arise when the participants begin experiencing how they themselves can direct their learning.

It is not least when teachers dare to venture out on this approach that I have experienced that the participants also plunge headlong into their chosen activities with an overwhelming enthusiasm, so that e.g. trivial questions about breaks, smoking, knocking-off time, etc. vanish into thin air; and the teachers whom participants were initially very sceptical toward are eventually considered "great".

However, the direct approach in connection with the issue of responsibility is neither always a possible option nor an appropriate one. It pre-supposes partly that it is quite clear in advance what the point of the course in question is, so the participants know what they must relate to, partly that the teachers have the self-confidence which is necessary for arguing and implementing this approach with the necessary combination of determination and understanding for the participants' reactions.

Therefore in most cases a more or less gradual approach is chosen, where the teachers at the outset accept considerable responsibility for the initiation of relevant activities and then gradually hand over more and more responsibility to the participants. Both teachers and participants as a rule feel most comfortable with this procedure, but experience shows that it also involves a certain risk that this hand over ends up taking much too long and is possibly never fully implemented.

It is thus important for the gradual approach, which in the specific case may be structured in numerous and very diverse fashions, that from the start it is presented and argued that such a gradual hand over of responsibility will take place and that there is a time schedule for the hand over which will be kept and which means that the participants fairly quickly will assume the responsibility for their own learning. As a rule of thumb, the hand over should be fully implemented not later than 1/3 into the course for short courses and not later than approximately one month into extended courses. Under all circumstances there must be time for the participants really to carry out significant sub-courses on their own re-sponsibility.

It is also important that the question of division of responsibility is addressed and discussed to a sufficient extent for the participants really to understand and accept it. The assumption of responsibility is the most essential function of any adult education: that one has precisely not been returned back to school, but been placed into a context where there are many opportunities and support for acquiring something that one desires to learn.

It is, as mentioned earlier, my experience that the question of division of responsibility on the one hand is absolutely vital for adult education programmes to be able in practice to strengthen the participants as per-sons. On the other hand there are so many and powerful forces both within the participants, within the teachers and in the environment that pull in the opposite direction, that it is necessary to pay very great attention to and show firmness in this area. It is naturally also of vital importance if there is to be development of competences and resistancy, because these concepts precisely contain very strong elements of self-confidence and self-direction.

14.3. Security and challenge

There may appear to be a contradiction between the strong demand for division of responsibility and the demand for a secure learning environment, which is an extension of the fact that competences and resistancy presuppose good conditions for accommodative and transformative processes.

The contradiction is, however, only apparent. Fundamentally, there is greater security in directing one's own learning and getting qualified support for learning than in being subjected to outside control. But often wishful thinking about the secure childhood school situation with its paternal or maternal teacher figure can prove an obstacle, and the adult education participants immediately slip into the expectation of child-like security even though in other areas they are used to experiencing adult security by assuming control of their situation.

This duality, which keeps appearing as an immediate condition in adult education programmes, places demands on the teacher and the institutions for being able to create fundamental security while at the same time maintaining that the responsibility for learning must lie with or be transferred to the participants. Again the pivotal point lies in presenting these matters and explaining and discussing them carefully, with kindness, empathy and firmness. Openness, kindness, personal commitment and a clear framework are important elements for the ability to develop security. The participants must feel secure as to where the teachers stand and that they can get support and backing, feel that there is no such thing as "stupid" or wrong questions, and that they are taken seriously just as they are.

One of the advantages of the learning that takes place in formalised education, seen e.g. in relation to learning in working life or everyday life, is that formal education is able to establish a protected space in which it is possible to experiment and make mistakes, and where one may get qualified and loyal help. This can provide the possibility for transcending learning processes that can be too risky for the participants in other contexts.

It is in practice to a very high degree the teachers who are the vital determinant for the development of such security, but the preconditions, e.g. with regard to the external framework, assessment forms and the participants' relation to the course in question may be very different. One of the most important elements is the participants' experience of the teachers as persons and their relationship to themselves as participants. It is important that the teachers appear as "whole" humans with feelings, opinions and commitment, and with relevant academic competences and a fundamental solidarity with the participants. Some of this is inherent in the concepts of the authentic and professional teacher. Teachers must be themselves and acknowledge their role as teacher (and not just as teacher or representative of a subject).

Security in the learning environment is thus of key importance; it is important that the group and the teacher get along and feel good, but the participants are also there to learn and develop. Therefore security must of necessity consist of more than mere congeniality. It must also include a mutual seriousness, a certainty that the parties take each other and the education seriously. For the participants it is an important element of security that it also includes an experience that they are presented with challenges that are significant and relevant.

For some adult education programme participants there are only problems in all this if the learning environment begins to crack or disintegrate. These are the ones who know what they want and go direct to the matter. However, most are more insecure and need help to discover what really means something to them. Here the teachers may play an important role as facilitators by adopting a listening attitude, showing empathy, being expectant and applying their experience and academic insight as sparring partners for the participants in their attempts to reach clarification. Teachers act as counsellors when uncertain and fumbling initiatives are to be translated into concrete activities at a suitable level that stretch-es the prior abilities of the various participants to the limit.

In the pedagogical direction which, based on the work of the Russians Lev Vygotsky and Aleksei Leontjev, is known as activity theory, there is a central concept concerning the students' zone of proximal development (Vygotsky 1978, 1986, Engeström 1987, 1993). It has been developed in relation to children, and one may have a certain measure of apprehension in this context (Illeris 2002, p. 54f), but in connection with adults who are themselves able to make key decisions on where they want to go, it may be a useful supporting concept to consider.

In any event, the duality of security and challenge is part of what most basically characterises a good adult education environment, and it is the task of institutions and teachers to develop it in concrete terms in relation to the participant groups they address. Not all participants are immedi-ately ready to play along with such a process, but almost all will react pos-itively if it is successfully established.

14.4. Activity

The mentioned activity theory approach is directly related to the concept of activity in education programmes. The concern is that the participants themselves are to be active in order for learning to take place, and it is quite fundamental that the concept of activity is taken in a broad sense and not merely a motor activity, i.e. if it is also considered to be activity to read a book, watch a video or think and reflect.

Here one must, however, show some care because there is almost no limit to what may pass for activity. One may well sit and stare at a TV set without this psychologically being called an activity, and one may also be employed on an entirely routine basis with many things while the mind has been switched on stand-by. Therefore activity theoreticians point out that the activity must be defined as a *goal-directed* activity – and it is e.g. not a focused activity to listen to a teacher indulging in hermeneutic meandering if one is completely uninterested in the subject of the text.

In adult education programmes the participants' activities are also of decisive importance, but here it is important that the concept is understood in relation to the fact that the concern is adults learning, and being an adult is concerned with controlling and taking responsibility for one's actions. Therefore the concept of activity in adult education programmes must be understood in the sense that it is concerned with broadly engaging in actions which are goal-directed and in which the participant takes part in choosing and directing, for this is where one learns in earnest. Therefore it is also vital for adult education programmes, and the institutions' and the teachers' task to see to it, that there are diverse opportunities for relevant participant activities, encouragement to commitment to them and possibilities for obtaining help and backing.

In this connection it is generally important that there is access to facilities and workshops where students can work with various media and materials, that there are relevant book collections, videos, Internet access and other possibilities for obtaining input, and opportunities for going out into the world outside the institution and gathering information and impressions, that there are e.g. offers of organised excursions, contact with relevant environments, etc.

14.5. Collectivity and individuality

There are many good reasons for emphasising collectivity in adult education programmes. Cooperation, collectivity and social responsibility were set up as overall important general goals in chapter 5, which can contribute to development of competences and resistancy. More specifically, collectivity is to a high degree able to contribute to a good learning environment, and group work of various kinds can directly promote the participants' learning processes. One may thus on the day-to-day level work with collectivity at two levels: partly at team or class level, partly at group level concerning specific work processes, including i.a. tasks and projects.

The collectivity at class level is not only important for the learning environment as such. It is also today for many adults of great importance at a more general level to be part of a committing and loyal collectivity as a counter-weight to the general individualisation trend and the fact that more and more adults live alone or in steadily diminishing family units.

For courses of slightly longer duration, the team can develop the character of a community of practice with vital impact on the social learning as this is described first and foremost by Etienne Wenger (1998). Therefore it is important to spend time and energy on development of collectivity, not least in the beginning phase of such an education programme.

The collectivity at group level around certain short and extended courses is, in addition, important both for training of the ability to co-operate and for the personal and the academic content learning. In groups one can partly handle greater challenges than one can handle alone, and partly one can learn surprisingly much from working together on various things, get one's suggestions and ideas commented on by others, listen to the others' initiatives and carry out various activities together.

I shall not here go into detail with the different forms of cooperation that may be put to use in adult education programmes. Here, I shall merely maintain as something very important for institutionalised adult education that the possibilities for binding cooperation in connection with learning are used.

However, at the same time it must also be pointed out that many adults may need to test their strength by completing a learning process alone and on their own premises. Self-containment was also one of the general goals set up for learning in chapter 5. Especially for adults who do not have much experience with education, it may be a great experience and strengthening of their self-confidence to handle a learning process on their own, and it can easily be combined directly with group and joint activities, e.g. through subsequent exchange of experience and comments on each other's course work.

14.6. Reflection and reflexivity

Finally, I also find it important to point out the significance that adult education programmes set the stage for and provide time and space for the participants' reflection on their own learning and their reflexive position on the learning's personal significance to them. Reflection and re-flexivity are especially important precisely in connection with development of competences and resistancy, and it is hardly mere coincidence that, parallel with the development of interest in the competence concept, there has been a corresponding development of the interest for reflection and reflexivity as important elements in and tools for creating a connection between the academic learning and its personal significance and application possibilities. A number of significant works within the field of education research in the broadest sense have in recent years in very different ways focused on these topics (e.g. Schön 1983, 1987, 1991, Mezirow 1991, Giddens 1990, 1991, Brookfield 1995).

Generally, reflection means afterthought, and I have previously described it as an accommodative oriented learning course that takes place staggered in time in relation to the impulses on which it builds (Illeris 2002, p. 45ff). Reflection consists in trying to think through an event or a course with care and consider its meaning after the event or course have been put at a distance, and it can typically lead to a learning which is more far-reaching and general than what one immediately gained from the experience when it unfolded. In addition, one can also, both immediately and in connection with the reflection, process one's experiences reflexively, i.e. put them in relation to oneself, one's learning course, one's perceptions, feelings and opinions (Illeris 2002, p. 90ff).

Reflection and reflexivity occur all the time, but it is important in terms of learning that these processes in institutionalised education courses can be implemented more systematically, e.g. if keeping a diary is part of the course, as has become increasingly common in many parts of the education system and in some cases is a direct requirement. However, it is also important that these processes are not only perceived and implemented as something individual. The collective reflection and reflexivity in groups and on teams can add important dimensions, e.g. response from others, and they can make the processes broader and placed in more perspective while at the same time they take them beyond the ordinary and limiting tendency to individualisation of late modernity.

It is also part of the functions of the institutions and the teachers in connection with adult education to ensure that there is time and room for systematic and deep reflection and reflexivity. In practice, it typically assumes the form of what was previously called formative (running) and summative (concluding) internal evaluation, which not so much are concerned with assessment as precisely the sharing of experience, reflection and forward-looking perspective, like e.g. in the mentioned review of a project course (cf. chapter 13.2).

14.7. Monitoring and evaluation

Parallel with and at the end of education courses there is, as a rule, one or more forms of monitoring and evaluation of the participants' activities and qualifications. Such monitoring and evaluation is in its source and essence a societal necessity; society must ensure that persons have specific skills to handle specific functions or be accepted into further education. At the same time, it can have great significance for the individual to get qualifications formally approved, practically, as concerns status and psychologically as an acknowledgement that can give identity and generate self-confidence.

However, it is also well known that monitoring and evaluation may have a very forceful and controlling influence on the education course and on the behaviour and consciousness of both participants and teachers in connection with a course, into the smallest details. Within adult education programmes, many and very diverse monitoring and evaluation forms are practised in relation to the participants. One of the important results of my research in Danish adult education is concerned with the participants' attitudes to these matters.

Generally, it is today the common attitude among adult education participants in Denmark that they would like to have documentation for completed education programmes, which not only testify to satisfactory participation, but also includes a certification of the qualifications they have acquired. With this, they also show willingness to accept that as a participant one must have one's qualifications tested, but there is widespread scepticism towards having this take place through an examination in the traditional sense. Many participants have painful experiences with taking exams, and indicate, among other things, that it involves heavy and irrelevant psychological pressure, that the evaluation is unfair, that too much depends on luck and coincidence, etc.

In addition to this, there is generally very great dissatisfaction with any kind of attendance records, at least if there also are exams or another form of qualitative evaluation. Attendance monitoring is typically perceived as the most obvious expression of the imposed child-role and disempowerment inherent in "returning to school". Adults are well able themselves to figure out what they must participate in and what they can do without, they are able themselves to take responsibility for prioritising their activities, and the important thing must be that they acquire the competences they are expected to gain.

It is, though, not easy for the participants to give clear expression to possible alternative ways to monitor and evaluate, as must be done in order to make it possible to document the competences acquired. However, it is a widely held view that evaluation must be carried out by the teachers with whom the students have daily contact, because regardless of the fact that there are both good and less good teachers, it is only they who have a background for knowing what the student actually knows and is able to do and understand. Furthermore, it is only in exceptional cases where the focus is on highly specific practical skills that a test or exam is relevant. In most cases by far, the participants want the evaluation to be made on the basis of the daily work and the small and major assignments and projects that form part of the course.

Based on the assumption that participants are responsible adults and that the aim of the education programmes is generally concerned with the development of competences and resistancy, there is every reason to respect the attitudes here expressed. In terms of learning, the concern is to find monitoring and evaluation forms that support, and not inhibit, the participants' independence, responsibility, cooperation, etc., and thereby also their competence development.

The traditional monitoring and evaluation forms must be considered an obsolete reflection of industrial society. With attendance monitoring and exams, the participants are placed in opposition to the "system" as a powerful adversary in the same way as in the labour conditions seen in industrial employment. The concern here is conformity and submission to external power-based demands and not the joint promotion of personal development and getting a realistic evaluation of it.

Naturally, the power aspect cannot be eliminated, but it is not impossible to find forms in which it assumes a less dominant character and to a higher degree respects the adult participants' experience, also even though they experience a certain duality between wish for self-direction and the wish for obtaining formal approval.

15. Councelling

In this chapter a number of matters are taken up that lie outside of or in the periphery of adult education study programmes themselves, but which nevertheless are of great importance to many participants with respect to their education and learning. These comprise the referral and counselling that take place before adult education commences, reception at the educational institutions, and the counselling options that exist – or do not exist – at the institutions in connection with the educational activities. From the point of view of the participants, there are very great deficiencies in these functions – deficiencies that would seem to have their background in a shortage of funds, but which, apart from difficult and humiliating experiences for the participants, also easily lead to greater expenses in other ways, for example when participants embark upon a course of study with bad motivation and negative expectations.

15.1. Placement or clarification in referral

It is only a minor proportion of the participants in adult education today who attend at their own initiative. The majority have been placed, referred or sent to attend the education programme in question, either by public authorities or agencies or by an employer. This placement may be made more or less with or against the individual's own will and interest, it may be made with or without more superficial or careful interviews and negotiations with the individual, and it may be made with or without various information to the individual on the contents and aim of the education, and reasons why the individual is referred to this specific education programme.

In our research it was probably the most obvious and urgent experience for us to observe the size of the proportion of the participants in the broad Danish adult education programmes who feel uncertain why they are enrolled in that particular education programme, and who, when the course starts, are not informed of the aim and point of the education and where it might possibly lead them. Our project did not carry out censuses or other forms of quantitative surveys, and there is also a very blurred distinction that makes it impossible to state with adequate precision the number of participants "who know what they are to do or want to do with their education". However, we could observe that at many educational institutions it was quite common that more than half of the participants at the entry level felt "placed", and had no reasonable prior knowledge of what the course aimed to achieve (cf. Illeris 2003a).

Part of the background for this is without doubt that the referring instances work under considerable time pressure and are subject to very tight limits as to the amount of time allowed to be allocated for each client. The outcome is quite generally that these instances are forced to consider their task completed as soon as a client has admitted into an education programme (or has got a job).

This situation is, however, doubly disempowering for the participants: first, they feel that they are under compulsion or pressure when they approach these authorities, and second, they feel that then they are not even shown reasonable individual concern, i.e. especially that they get too little information and too little time for considering and influencing their placement. Something similar often also happens when private and public employers send their employees with brief schooling on a course.

It is immediately clear that in such a context, it is rather incidental and uncertain if appropriate learning in the education course will even start, and it becomes even more paradoxical if one relates it to modern requirements for competence development and for what I have written in earlier chapters on when and how adults become part of appropriate learning processes. On top of this comes that their frustrations can be a heavy force for disintegration in the education programme, so that it also falls apart for other participants who started with a more positive and focused approach, something which we could clearly observe in classes that involved many participants with this feeling of being placed.

15.2. Counselling before the course of studies

It is immediately apparent from the previous section that many participants in the broad Danish adult education programmes had not, prior to the start of their education course, received education counselling that they found satisfactory. Even though in most cases they are objectively in a situation where they need education, they experience subjectively that they have been subjected to compulsion and placement, and they find this humiliating and frustrating.

However, this is also inappropriate from the perspective of society and economy. In such cases it is actually only on paper (and in the statistics) that activation takes place. The motivation and personal "acceptance of the education" that are the preconditions for suitable and focused learning and competence development are, in such cases, entirely absent and instead there is insecurity, confusion, frustration, anger and other negative feelings. The time saved in the referring instance, which must be assumed to be the most important reason for the insufficient counselling, is thus countered by a waste of resources in the education institution, which may be many times larger and possibly even affect teachers and perhaps other participants. To the extent counselling takes place in such a way, we are looking at not merely what is ethically highly criticisable administration, but also a major error in economic terms.

For counselling in this context to be ethically defensible, practical and economically appropriate, it is of decisive importance that it is applied until the individual in question psychologically "accepts the education", i.e. has subjectively realised and accepted that the chosen education course is suitable for the individual in that situation and that therefore he or she will do the best to achieve the best possible result. Only then is it humanly and economically reasonable to begin the education.

Such an aim, let it be said, is by no means unrealistic. When we bear in mind the situation in which these individuals typically find themselves, suspended between the threat of societal marginalisation and the opportunity for a relevant upgrade or re-qualification, by far the majority of them will sooner or later decide to commit themselves to a meaningful education. In our research, almost all unemployed education programme participants stated that their greatest wish, the key element for them, was to get an acceptable job (and they were not particularly picky with regard to what they considered acceptable).

The precondition is, of course, first, that in the individual cases it is possible to find a realistic opportunity, but second, and equally important, that there is also time and support for the deep and personal adaptation process that is necessary. There is a need for a dialogue that takes its point of departure in the individuals' own premises. There is a need for time for the individuals to ponder the issues, discuss them with others with whom they feel confident, get used to the idea, find the subjectively positive aspects of the situation, and first and foremost accept entering actively and wholeheartedly into the project.

In our research it was an important and obvious observation that even though many were very dissatisfied with the process and certainly did not perceive it as something that had anything to do with counselling, they all, with a few exceptions, thought that the placement in which it had resulted was reasonable enough in spite of everything. However, they still experienced it as a placement, and this implied a humiliation and a negative attitude which they felt very deeply. All this "counselling" could obviously be carried through to a positive choice with relative ease and thereby a mental acceptance which psychologically would have given an entirely different entry situation to the education and thus also to the learning.

15.3. Reception at the educational institutions

No matter how the referral and counselling have been carried out, a new situation of great significance for the subsequent learning possibilities almost always appears in connection with the participants' first meeting with their educational institution and the start of their education programme. I have chosen to raise this issue in the present chapter because, like counselling, it lies just at the edge of the education course proper, but is nonetheless significant for the learning possibilities.

In the uncertain personal situation in which many of the participants find themselves, it is first and foremost important the individual participant experiences the meeting between the participants and the educational institution as secure, confidence-generating and directed towards a cooperation in which the participant gets support and real opportunities for personal development. Furthermore, given the counselling scenario outlined above, it must for the time being be considered realistic to assume that the participants need information on what the education is all about and where it can take the participants, as well as a number of practical matters concerning the general framework for the education programme.

Based on our observations and interviews, it is our impression that the educational institutions and teachers generally are aware of these matters and try to overcome them. All the same there may be serious problems because for some of the participants it is a very sensitive situation.

Especially the major educational institutions and centres often appear huge, impersonal and institution-like from their buildings alone, and a new and insecure participant can very easily feel very small, anonymous and insignificant. As many new classes also often start at the same time, there are crowds of people trying to find their way, and even though there are signs, the effect can be labyrinthine. Sometimes the new students meet for the first time at tables in a large canteen or hall, and even though there are signposts and coffee on the tables, it can seem very impersonal and overwhelming in the large room with poor acoustics.

Perhaps students could meet in smaller rooms, perhaps classes could start staggered at half-hour intervals, perhaps teachers could appear fifteen minutes early, perhaps there could be people posted at the entrance that one might ask practical questions. Much could be done with small means to deal with this difficult situation if there is real comprehension of the magnitude of the impact it may have, especially on the participants with the weakest prior qualifications.

One important point is the way in which the teacher opens the session when the students have entered the room where the course activities are to take place. There seems here to be a tendency to start with the practical information first, possibly after a short round of presentations, which is nearly a "shout-your-name" round. It is so wonderfully concrete, but it is also very impersonal. The message easily becomes the one that, "here we have some rules which we must observe even though we are, of course, quite relaxed". In any event, the participants are thus placed as objects to the rules. Second, events implicitly establish a framework that essentially conveys the message that education is a duty and a burden; like in school and in traditional employment: the way to play the game is to get one's breaks and escape as early as possible.

All this is not in and of itself wrong, but in the situation it might be more appropriate to focus more on the participants and their situation, for instance that they are quickly placed in smaller groups where they can be active getting to know each other, and that the contents and opportunities offered by the education are presented and discussed, especially if many participants have insufficient prior information. For education that includes computers and workshops, many participants will also typically want to be very speedily introduced to the more tangible matters that have often been at the centre of their prior imaginations and expectations.

15.4. Counselling during the studies

During the education programme itself, an institutionalised counselling function is available at some adult education institutions. This counselling has, it is true, typically a primarily academic and study related aim, but during our research we have heard from many education participants at these institutions that they have also been able to use the counsellors for personal support, which many consider of great importance, especially in the difficult initial phase.

In most Danish adult education programmes, such counselling is, however, left to the individual teachers, and it appears to function in a rather random manner. There are without doubt many teachers who accept responsibility for such counselling, and much practical and repeated experience has shown me that counselling may be carried out in a splendid way in connection with ordinary tutorials. However, there is no instance that has it as its task, and therefore it is left to chance; the individuals in question might as well have been assigned to one of the other teachers who do not venture into this type of issue.

It is possible that it is the most appropriate solution that the referring authorities' counselling tasks finish when an acceptable place of education has been found and the further counselling is subsequently transferred to the educational institution. It is difficult to draw a general conclusion. Perhaps one option for a future arrangement might be to have such a counselling function at all adult education institutions. However, this must of course be done subject to the premise that the institutions have the obligation and resources to accept this task, that qualified counsellors are appointed or trained, and that the arrangement is independent of the general economic interests of the institutions, i.e. that counselling is financed independently and not through the institution's ordinary budget.

It is, however, quite certain that there is a need for formalised access and right to qualified study-related and personal counselling in connection with all adult education programmes, both because a very large part of the participants have a need for such counselling and because it can contribute to a more appropriate course of education for many. This would result in society therefore getting more and better learning and competence development. Effective student counselling will be able to "pick up" especially the participants who have the weakest prior qualifications and the biggest problems, and who are therefore also most exposed to the risk of dropping out without completing the course.

For precisely these participants, it is of great importance that there is a place where they can go and have a right to be, where they do not need to ask permission first, and where there is a person who is ready to help them and who does not limit the support provided to content matter, because this is always intertwined with personal affairs.

15.5. The way in

If one takes a more general look at the road into adult education as a whole, at the process that includes selection, preparation and the encounter with education programmes, it must first and foremost be maintained that the rather large share of participants we have encountered in Danish adult education programmes who are insecure and reluctant, who do not know why they are in the programme in question and what they are to or want to do with it, even well into the courses, are a sign that these processes in many cases have not functioned adequately seen from the participants' perspective.

In Denmark and other similar countries, it is especially the referral and counselling that are under severe time pressure and problematic. Excessive emphasis seems to be placed on swift and efficient placement, and much too little on the difficult psychological conversion process which it is for adults to have to embark on an education programme, often with a perspective which involves a substantial change of their personal and social situation.

The insufficient emphasis and effort in this area, when looked at from the participants' perspective, seem to be the greatest weakness to afflict the large-scale expansion of adult education programmes that has taken place. This is a weakness that not only means that the expansion has no effect on a large share of the participants, but also is to be criticised in terms of ethics. It involves extensive waste of both human and economic resources.

Part 4

Adult education programmes today

The concluding, fourth part of this book provides a brief summing up of the most important points of the previous chapters.

The summing up largely follows the structure of the book. It starts out on the general societal level with the slogans about lifelong learning and competence development. It moves on to the most important general characteristics of adult learning, continues with the general objectives and organisation of adult education programmes, and finishes with a series of conclusions about division of responsibility, forms of work, teacher functions and counselling.

The intention is to provide a relatively swift overview of the main points in the book. This, naturally, requires that the previous chapters of the book be read if a deeper understanding is to be achieved.

16. Summary

This final chapter summarises the most important points made in the book in a brief practice-oriented form. A point-by-point presentation with relatively short formulations has been employed to make the messages as clear as possible. This means, of course, that a great deal of the contents and argumentation of the book are lost. For this reason, the summary cannot stand alone but must be understood as part of the totality of the book.

16.1. Lifelong learning for all

The slogan about *lifelong learning for all* can be an important, up-to-date point of departure for the necessary placement and development of adult education programmes as a key function in late modern society, because this society is characterised by great changeability and varying opportunities, requiring that its members are able to readjust to a high degree.

In official national and supranational reports, the slogan is presented as a matter affecting the economic growth and competitiveness of society, social balance and cohesion, and the interests and life quality of citizens.

However, the policy pursued in the area rather unilaterally prioritises the economic objectives, while the targets at social and personal levels are largely overlooked or considered as being satisfied by means of the economically oriented policy.

This distorts the content of the slogan. It becomes subject to economic rationality with a mechanical and untenable perception of education and learning, and the aspects of adult education that should have to do with social community, cultural enrichment and personal development for the members of society, in many cases become adaptation, pressure and compulsion.

The slogan about lifelong learning is fast becoming an empty shell because learning is not taken seriously as a central, complex and demanding human function. If the positive signals of this slogan are to be maintained, improvements must be made in terms of practical policy in the possibilities of ordinary adults to take part in learning activities with which they can identify and in a number of social and personal aspects of the programmes.

16.2. Competences and resistancy

In parallel with the slogan about lifelong learning, a perception has developed to the effect that the necessary and desirable results of the learning activities should have the character of personal *competences*, i.e. not merely knowledge, skills and qualifications, but also the ability and the will to transfer them into appropriate actions in relation to relevant current and future situations and challenges.

At both national and supranational level, resources are invested in mapping and listing important competences, and a number of different proposals have been developed in this field. The effort, however, is concentrated in developing the competency approach as an instrument of management while the same attention does not seem to be paid to the way in which competences in practice can be acquired through education and learning.

There is tendency to view the competences on the basis of societal categories and needs, with the perspectives of the participants taking a back seat. In this area also, the societal and the participant oriented perspectives must be maintained in theory and practice if the concept of competence is to retain its positive, progressive content and its general legitimacy.

In addition, the types of competences figuring in the official lists have a tendency to overlook the fact that, fundamentally, late modern market society is based on competition and thus full of contradictions and conflicts. For this reason, account is not taken of both society and its members having a basic need for competences to acknowledge and tackle the numerous interest-determined influences we all receive and which, to a rising extent, have a professional, calculating nature designed by advertising agents and spin doctors and aiming precisely at an interest-determined impact.

Therefore, competency thinking must also include a dimension of critical opposition that has to do with the competence to hold on to independent orientations, social responsibility and the like, which this book summaries by the term of *resistancy*.

16.3. Adult learning and ambivalence

Therefore, in general in the organisation and practice of adult education programmes the slogan about lifelong learning must have to do with the development of relevant competences and resistancy.

From this perspective, it is of decisive importance to understand that fundamentally *adult learning* is characterised by being selective and self-directed. In other words, adults best learn what they find subjectively meaningful, either because it is something they want to learn or because it is something they experience as important or necessary for them to learn. On the other hand, adults are very little inclined to learn something the meaning of which they cannot see from their own perspective, or this learning becomes superficial and reluctant in nature, reducing its possibilities of application and its flexibility.

Positive learning is frequently also complicated in connection with an institutionalised educational situation, where it is mixed with the comprehensive socialisation to a pupil role which means, among other things, that control and responsibility is handed over to the institution and the teachers.

For this reason, but also because today adult education is marked more by outer necessity than by voluntary choice, participants in adult education to a high degree experience *ambivalence* and duality. Most of the participants both want and do not want to become engaged in the intended learning.

But if they experience that learning can take place on their own terms, a change can occur resulting in the ambivalence disappearing and the full learning potential expanding.

16.4. Division of responsibility

On the basis of both democratic and ethical ideals, and because adult learning functions far better under these conditions, it is crucial that the participants in adult education are consistently regarded and treated as independent and responsible adults. In other words, that within some broad, open frames and options they are able to and have the right and duty to themselves manage and take responsibility for their own learning.

Studies of the existing, broad Danish adult education programmes seen from the participants' point of view show that at present the programmes are rarely viewed in this way. The school management, the teachers and the participants themselves are basically inclined to reproduce the dependent pupil-teacher relationship that is so well known from childhood school.

A clear *division of responsibility* is thus the key to an adult education culture that is in accordance with the ideals of society and can form the framework of the effective and relevant development of competences and resistancy. This implies that institutions and the teachers responsible take care of the framework conditions and the organisation of relevant input and working opportunities, while the participants are responsible for their own learning and engagement.

What is paradoxical is that experience has shown that in this connection the institutions and teachers must also take responsibility for the participants being encouraged to and getting a genuine opportunity to take responsibility for their own learning. This seldom takes place without resistance on the part of the participants. But when they first experience and believe that they themselves are in control, a starting point has been created for effective and engaged learning.

16.5. Participant direction, problem orientation and differentiated activities

On the pedagogical level, it is important that the division of responsibility is in practice translated into real *participant direction*, i.e. that it is the participants who control the process in interaction with the teachers' qualified and loyal assistance and support.

There is, in addition, the principle of *problem orientation*, i.e. that the point of departure for the learning activities is taken in broadly defined thematic areas and problem fields that the participants find it important to work with in relation to the targets of their education programmes. This increases the possibilities for active, relevant learning.

With participant direction and problem orientation as the fundamental pedagogical principles, there is, however, nothing to stop the inclusion of courses that are teacher-controlled and substance oriented, in agreement with the participants.

"Pure" participant direction and problem orientation are best practised through project work. This means that, on the basis of the nature of the content and the participants' qualifications, the way is open for weighted interaction between different varieties of the four basic pedagogical forms of work: teaching, exercises, studies and projects.

Finally, it is important to create significant opportunities for trainee periods and practice learning in close interaction with the institutionally based form of work.

16.6. The tasks of the teachers

In adult education courses of the type outlined here, the teachers are professionally and pedagogically competent and loyal persons facilitating and supporting the participants' learning processes. There is no particular teacher role that fulfils this function best, and the most important thing is for the teachers themselves to develop a professional, authentic manner of functioning with which they feel comfortable.

As already mentioned, participant direction by no means implies that the teachers have less work or responsibility. First and foremost, one key task is to establish the division of responsibility and participant direction described. Over and above this, among other things a secure and challenging learning environment must be created, relevant types of activities must be found and academic input must be provided in accordance with the needs of the participants and adjusted to other sides of the programme, a fruitful community must be created at the same time as the individual participant is supported in suitable ways, and space and routines must be created for reflection and reflexivity that ensures that the learning interacts with the interests and qualifications of the individual participant. All this must take place in ongoing interaction with the participants themselves controlling their own learning processes.

Finally, and somewhat contradictorily, it is usually necessary that the teachers also take on the societally necessary control and evaluation function that ensures that the participants receive formal recognition of their learning.

16.7. Counselling

From the point of view of the participants, the counselling before and during courses of adult education would seem to be the most criticizable element in the overall profile of the programmes.

In particular, the preliminary referral and counselling - irrespective of the context in which this takes place – are experienced as very unsatisfactory and to a higher degree as placement than real counselling. There are shocking numbers of participants in the broad adult education programmes in Denmark who have no clear idea of what their education programme is about and contains or why they are there in the first place.

The most urgent reform that can make the reality of the adult education programmes approach the ideals of lifelong learning and competence development must ensure that the preliminary process becomes genuine counselling that leads to the participants subjectively choosing and accepting the education in question and thus being ready to take responsibility for their own activity and learning.

In addition, in connection with the start and the remainder of the programmes there is a need for an ongoing, independent counselling service concerning educational as well as personal matters. Most of the participants today are in the broad adult education programmes because they need to readjust and get further. This very often has to do with changes in well-established identities and these are demanding processes where both the individual and society are best served when qualified support is provided.

References

Adorno, Theodor W. (1971): *Erziehung zur Mündigkeit*. [Upbringing for personal authority]. Frankfurt a.M.: Suhrkamp.

Andersen, Anders Siig (2002): *Mellem velstand og velfærd – uddannelsesreformer i et risikoperspektiv*. [Between prosperity and welfare – educational reforms in a risk perspective]. Roskilde: The adult education research group, Roskilde University.

Andersen, Vibeke – Illeris, Knud (1995): *Når skolekulturer samarbejder*. [When school cultures co-operate]. Copenhagen: The Danish Labour Market Authority & Danish Ministry of Education.

Andersen, Vibeke – Illeris, Knud – Kjærsgaard, Christian – Larsen, Kirsten – Olesen, Henning Salling – Ulriksen, Lars (1994): *Qualifications and living people*. Roskilde: The adult education research group, Roskilde University.

Andersen, Vibeke – Illeris, Knud – Kjærsgaard, Christian – Larsen, Kirsten – Olesen, Henning Salling – Ulriksen, Lars (1996): *General Qualification*. Roskilde: The adult education research group, Roskilde University.

Anderson, M.L. – Lindeman, Eduard C. (1927): *Education Through Experience*. New York: Workers' Education Bureau.

Antikainen, Ari (1998): In Search of the Meaning and Practice of Life-Long Learning. In Knud Illeris (ed): *Adult Education in a Transforming Society*. Copenhagen: Roskilde University Press.

Antikainen, Ari – Kauppila, Juha (2000): The Story of a Learner – Educational Generations and the Future of Liberal Adult Education in Finland. In Knud Illeris (ed): *Adult Education in the Perspective of the Learners*. Copenhagen: Roskilde University Press.

Argyris, Chris (2000): *The Next Challenge in Organizational Learning, Leadership and Change*. Paper presented at the Learning Lab Denmark opening conference, Copenhagen, 6 November.

Argyris, Chris – Schön, Donald A. (1996): *Organizational Learning II – Theory, Method, Practice*. Reading, Mass.: Addison-Wesley.

Badcock, Christopher (1988): *Essential Freud: A Modern Introduction to Classical Psychoanalysis.* Oxford: Blackwell.

Beck, Ulrich (1992 [1986]): *Risk Society: Towards a New Modernity.* London: SAGE.

Becker-Schmidt, Regina (1987): Dynamik sozialen Lernens. [Dynamics of social learning]. In Regina Becker-Schmidt & Gudrun-Axeli Knapp: *Geschlechtertrennung – Geschlechterdifferenz – Suchbewegungen sozialen Lernens.* [Gender division – gender difference – search movements of social learning]. Bonn: J.H.W. Dietz Nachf.

Berliner, Peter – Berthelsen, Jens (1989): Passiv aggression [Passive aggression]. *Nordisk Psykologi,* 4, 301-315.

Bild, Tage – Jørgensen, Henning – Lassen, Morten – Madsen, Morten (1993): *Fællesskab og forskelle.* [Community and differences] Aalborg: CARMA, Aalborg University.

Billett, Stephen (2001): *Learning in the Workplace:* Strategies for Effective Practice. Crows Nest, NSW: Allen & Unwin.

Bjørnåvold, Jens (2000): *Making Learning Visible.* Thessaloniki: CEDE-FOP.

Boud, David (2003): *Combining Work and Learning: The Disturbing Challenge of Practice.* Keynote speech given at the CRLL Conference: Experiential – Community – Workbased: Researching Learning Outside the Academy. Glasgow Caledonian University, 27-29 June.

Bourdieu, Pierre (1998 [1994]): *Practical Reason: On the Theory of Action.* Cambridge, UK: Polity Press.

Bramming, Pia (2003): Kompetence er der masser af! [There is a lot of competence!] *Uddannelse,* 1, 16-22.

Brookfield, Stephen D. (1987): *Developing Critical Thinkers.* Milton Keynes: Open University Press.

Brookfield, Stephen D. (1990): *The Skilful Teacher.* San Francisco: Jossey-Bass.

Brookfield, Stephen D. (1995): *Becoming a Critically Reflective Teacher.* San Francisco: Jossey-Bass.

Brookfield, Stephen D. (2000): Adult cognition as a dimension of lifelong learning. In John Field & Mal Leicester (eds): *Lifelong Learning – Education Across the Lifespan.* London: Routledge-Falmer.

CEDEFOP (2001): *Training and learning for competence.* Luxembourg: European Communities.

CEDEFOP (2003): *Learning for employment. Second report on vocational education and training policy in Europe. Executive summary.* Luxembourg: European Communities.

Christiansen, Frederik Voetmann (1999): Exemplarity and educational planning. In Henning Salling Olesen & Jens Højgaard Jensen (eds): *Project Studies – A Late Modern University Reform?* Copenhagen: Roskilde University Press.

Coffield, Frank (2003): The holes in the heart of current policies on lifelong learning. In CEDEFOP: *Policy, Practice and Partnership: Getting to Work on Lifelong Learning.* Thessaloniki: CEDEFOP.

Colley; Helen – Hodkinson, Phil – Malcolm, Janice (2003): *Informality and Formality in Learning.* London: Learning and Skills Research Centre.

Commission of the European Communities (2000): *A Memorandum on Lifelong Learning.* Brussels: European Commission.

Commission of the European Communities (2002): *Investing Efficiently in Education and Training: An Imperative for Europe.* Brussels: European Commission.

Cooper, Paul – McIntyre, Donald (1996): *Effective Teaching and Learning: Teachers' and Students' Perspective.* Buckingham: Open University Press.

Corder, Nicholas (2002): *Learning to Teach Adults:* An Introduction. London: Routledge/Falmer.

Damasio, Antonio R. (1994): *Descartes' Error: Emosion, Reason and the Human Brain.* New York: Grosset/Putnam.

Damasio, Antonio R. (1999): *The Feelings of What Happens: Body, Emotion and the Making of Consciousness.* London: Vintage.

Danish Ministry of Education (1996): *Livslang uddannelse for alle.* [Lifelong education for all]. Copenhagen: Undervisningsministeriet.

Danish Ministry of Education (2002): *Voksenuddannelse i tal 2002.* [Adult education in figures]. Copenhagen: Undervisningsministeriet.

Darkenwald, Gordon G. (1987): Assessing the Social Environment of Adult Classes. *Studies in the Education of Adults,* 19, 127-136.

Darkenwald, Gordon G. (1989): Enhancing the Adult Classroom Environment. In Elisabeth Hayes (ed): *Effective Teaching Styles*. San Francisco: Jossey-Bass.

Davonport, Joseph (1993 [1987]): Is there any way out of the andragogy morass? In Mary Thorpe, Richard Edwards & Ann Hanson (eds): *Culture and Processes of Adult Learning*. London: Routledge.

DeSeCo (2001): *12 Countries Contributing to DeSeCo – A Summary Report*. Neuchâtel: University of Neuchâtel on behalf of Swiss Federal Statistics Office.

Dewey, John (1916): *Democracy and Education*. New York: Macmillan.

Dewey, John (1934): The way out of educational confusion. In Reginald D. Archambault (ed): *John Dewey on Education – Selected Writings*. Chicago: University of Chicago Press.

Dillenbourg, Pierre (1999): What do you mean by callaborative learning. In Pierre Dillenbourg (ed): *Collaborative Learning – Cognitive and Computational Approaches*. Elsvier Science.

Dirckinck-Holmfeld, Lone (1990): *Kommunikation på trods og på tværs. Projektpædagogik og datamatkonferencer i fjernundervisning*. [Communication in defiance and across. Project studies and computer conferences in distance education]. Aalborg: PICNIC-nyt, 9, Aalborg University.

Dirckinck-Holmfeld, Lone – Fibiger, Bo (eds) (2002): *Learning in Virtual Environments*. Copenhagen: Samfundslitteratur.

Dominicé, Pierre (2000): *Learning from Our Lives – Using Educational Biographies with Adults*. San Francisco: Jossey-Bass.

Dreyfus, Hubert – Dreyfus, Stuart (1986): *Mind over Machine*. New York: Free Press.

Elkjær, Bente (2002): E-læring på arbejdspladsen. [E-learning in the workplace]. In Knud Illeris (ed): *Udspil om læring i arbejdslivet*. [Initiatives on workplace learning]. Copenhagen: Roskilde University Press.

Engeström, Yrjö (1987): *Learning by Expanding: An Activity-Theoretical Approach to Developmental Research*. Helsinki: Orienta-Kunsultit.

Engeström, Yrjö (1993): Developmental studies of work as a testbench of activity theory. In Seth Chaikling & Jean Lave (eds): *Understanding*

Practice – Perspectives on Activity and Context. New York: Cambridge University Press.

Erikson, Erik H. (1968): *Identity, Youth and Crises*. New York: Norton.

Faure, Edgar – et al. (1972): *Learning to Be*. Paris: UNESCO.

Fenger-Grøn, Carsten – Kristiansen, Jens Erik (red)(2001): *Kritik af den økonomiske fornuft*. [Critique of economical reason]. Copenhagen: Reitzel.

Festinger, Leon (1957): *A Theory of Cognitive Dissonance*. Stanford: Stanford University Press.

Field, John (2002): *Lifelong Learning and the New Educational Order*. Stoke-on-Trent: Trentham Books, 2. edition.

Flavell, John H. (1963): *The Developmental Psychology of Jean Piaget*. New York: Van Nostrand.

Foucault, Michel (1977 [1975]): *Discipline and Punish: The Birth of the Prison*. New York: Pantheon.

Freire, Paulo (1970): *Pedagogy of the Oppressed*. New York: Seabury.

Freud, Anna (1942 [1936]): *The Ego and the Mechanisms of Defence*. London: Hogarth Press.

Furth, Hans G. (1987): *Knowledge as Desire*. New York: Columbia University Press.

Garrick, John (1998): *Informal learning in the Workplace:* Unmasking Human Resource Development. London: Routledge.

Gergen, Kenneth J. (1994): *Realities and Relationships*. Cambridge, Mass.: Harvard University Press.

Giddens, Anthony (1990): *The Consequences of Modernity*. Stanford: Stanford University Press.

Giddens, Anthony (1991): *Modernity and Self-Identity*. Cambridge, UK: Polity Press.

Giroux, Henry A. (2001): *Theory and Resistance in Education:* Towards a Pedagogy for the Opposition. Westport, Connecticut: Birgin & Garvey, 2. edition.

Guilford, John P. (1967): *The Nature of Human Intelligence*. New York: McGraw-Hill).

Hake, Barry (1999): Lifelong learning in late modernity: The challenges to society, organizations, and individuals. *Adult Education Quarterly*, 2

(49), 79-91.

Hartree J. (1984): Malcolm Knowles' Theory of Andragogy: *A Critique*. *International Journal of Lifelong Education*, 3 (3), 203-210.

Huisken, Freerk (1972): *Zur Kritik bürgerlicher Didaktik und Bildungsökonomie*. [To the critique of bourgeois didactics and educational economy]. München: Paul List Verlag.

Illeris, Knud (1974): *Problemorientering og deltagerstyring. Oplæg til en alternativ didaktik*. [Problem orientation and participant direction: a proposal of an alternative educational theory]. Copenhagen: Munksgaard.

Illeris, Knud (1981): *Modkvalificeringens pædagogik*. [Pedagogy of counterqualification]. Copenhagen: Unge Pædagoger.

Illeris, Knud (1995): *Læring, udvikling og kvalificering*. [Learning, development and qualification]. Roskilde: The adult education research group, Roskilde University.

Illeris, Knud (1998): *Adult Learning and Responsibility*. In Knud Illeris (ed): Adult Education in a Transforming Society. Copenhagen: Roskilde University Press.

Illeris, Knud (1999): Project work in university studies: Background and current issues. In Henning Salling Olesen & Jens Højgaard Jensen (eds): *Project studies – A Late Modern University Reform?* Copenhagen: Roskilde University Press.

Illeris, Knud (2000): *Voksenuddannelse som masseuddannelse – disciplinering til fleksibilitet*. [Adult education as mass education – disciplining for flexibility]. Copenhagen: Roskilde University Press.

Illeris, Knud (2002 [1999]): *The Three Dimensions of Learning*. Copenhagen: Roskilde University Press / Leicester, UK: NIACE.

Illeris, Knud (2003a): Adult Education as Experienced by the Learners. *International Journal of Lifelong Education*, 22 (1), 13-23.

Illeris, Knud (2003b): Learning Changes through Life. *Lifelong Learning in Europe*, 8 (1), 51-60.

Illeris, Knud (2003c): *Workplace Learning and Learning Theory*. Journal of Workplace Learning, 15 (4), 167-178.

Illeris, Knud (2003d): Towards a Contemporary and Comprehensive Theory of Learning. *International Journal of Lifelong Education*, 22

(4), 411-421.

Illeris, Knud (2003e): Learning, Identity and Self-Orientation in Youth. *Young – Nordic Journal of Youth Research,* 11 (4), 357-376.

Illeris, Knud (2003f): Low Skilled Adults' Motivation for Learning. In CEDEFOP: *Policy, Practice and Partnership: Getting to Work on Lifelong Learning.* Thessaloniki: CEDEFOP.

Illeris, Knud (2004): Transformative Learning in the Persapective of a Comprehensive Learning Theory. *Journal of Transformative Education.*

Illeris, Knud – Andersen, Vibeke – Kjærsgaard, Christian – Larsen, Kirsten – Olesen, Henning Salling – Ulriksen, Lars (1995): *Almenkvalificering.* [General qualification]. Roskilde: The adult education research group, Roskilde University.

Illeris, Knud – Katznelson, Noemi – Simonsen, Birgitte – Ulriksen, Lars (2002): *Ungdom, identitet og uddannelse.* [Youth, identity and education]. Copenhagen: Roskilde University Press.

Jansen, Theo – Finger, Mathias – Wildemeersch, Danny (1998): Lifelong Learning for Responsibility: Exploring the Significance of Aesthetic Rationality for Adult Education. In John Holford – Peter Jarvis – Colin Griffin (eds): *International Perspectives on Lifelong Learning.* London: Kogan Page.

Jarvis, Peter (1992): *Paradoxes of Learning: On Becoming an Individual in Society.* San Francisco: Jossey-Bass.

Jarvis, Peter (2001): *Learning in Later Life.* London: Kogan Page.

Jarvis, Peter (2002): *The Implications of Life-Wide Learning for Lifelong Learning.* Paper presented at the Danish EU Presidency Conference, Elsinore, 9.10.

Jarvis, Peter – Holford, John – Griffin, Colin (1998): *The Theory and Practice of Learning.* London: Kogan Page.

Jensen, Johan Fjord (1993): *Livsbuen – voksenpsykologi og livsaldre.* [The life arch: adult psychology and life ages]. Copenhagen: Gyldendal.

Journal of Nordic Educational Research (1997): *Apprenticeship –Learning and Social Practice.* Special Issue, 17 (3).

Jørgensen, Per Schultz (1999): Hvad er kompetence? [What is competence?] *Uddannelse,* 9, 4-13.

Jørgensen, Per Schultz (2001): Kompetence – overvejelser over et begreb.

[Competence – considerations on a concept]. *Nordisk Psykologi*, 3, 181-208.

Kant, Immanuel (1998 [1781]): *The Critique of Pure Reason*. Cambridge Mass.: Cambridge University Press.

Kern, Horst – Schumann, Michael (1970): *Industriearbeit und Arbeiterbewusstsein*. [Industrial work and worker consciousness]. Frankfurt a.M.: Europäische Verlagsanstalt.

Kilpatrick, William H. (1918): The project method – The use of purposeful act in the educative process. *Teachers College Record*, 19, 319-335.

Knowles, Malcolm S. (1970): *The Modern Practice of Adult Education – Andragogy Versus Pedagogy*. New York: Association Press.

Knowles, Malcolm S. (1973): *The Adult Learner: A Neglected Species*. Houston: Gulf Publishing.

Knowles, Malcolm S. (1975): *Self-directed Learning: A Guide for Learners and Teachers*. Chicago: Follet Publishers.

Knowles, Malcolm S. et al. (1984): *Andragogy in Action*. San Francisco: Jossey-Bass.

Kolb, David A. (1984): *Experiential Learning*. Englewood Cliffs: Prentice Hall.

Korsgaard, Ove (1997): *Kampen om lyset – dansk voksenoplysning gennem 500 år*. [The struggle about the light – Danish adult enlightenment through 500 years]. Copenhagen: Gyldendal.

Lassen, Morten (2000): VEU-lovgivning eller VEU-reform? [Adult and continuing education legislation or adult and continuing education reform? *Dansk Pædagogisk Tidsskrift*, 1, 56-73.

Lave, Jean – Wenger, Etienne (1991): *Situated Learning: Legitimate Peripheral Participation*. New York: Cambridge University Press.

LeDoux, Joseph (2002): *Synaptic Self: How Our Brains Become Who We Are. New York:* Viking Penguin.

Leithäuser, Thomas (1976): *Formen des Alltagsbewusstseins*. [The forms of everyday consciousness]. Frankfurt a.M.: Campus.

Leithäuser, Thomas (1992): Teorien om hverdagsbevidstheden i dag. [The theory of everyday consciousness today]. *Unge Pædagoger*, 7-8, 45-56.

Leithäuser, Thomas (2000): Subjectivity, Lifeworld and Work Organization. In Knud Illeris (ed): *Adult Education in the Perspective of the Learners.* Copenhagen: Roskilde University Press.

Mager, Robert F. (1961): On the Sequencing of Instructional Content. Southern University Press: *Psychological Reports,* 9, 405-413.

Masuch, Michael (1972): *Uddannelsessektorens politiske økonomi.* [The political economy of the education sector]. Reinbek: Rowohlt.

Merleau-Ponty, Maurice (1970 [1945]): *Phenomenology of Perception.* London: Routledge & Kegan.

Merriam, Sharan B. – Caffarella, Rosemary S. (1999): *Learning in Adulthood – A Comprehensive Guide.* San Francisco: Jossey-Bass, 2. edition.

Mezirow, Jack (1990): How Critical Reflection Triggers Transformative Learning. In Jack Mezirow et al.: *Fostering Critical Reflection in Adulthood.* San Francisco: Jossey-Bass.

Mezirow, Jack (1991): *Transformative Dimensions of Adult Learning.* San Francisco: Jossey-Bass.

Nielsen, Birger Steen – Nielsen, Kurt Aagaard – Olsén, Peter (1996): Al den snak om livslang uddannelse. [All that talk about education]. *Dansk pædagogisk tidsskrift,* 2, 29-36.

Nielsen, Jørgen Lerche – Webb, Thomas W. (1999): Project Work at the Reform University of Roskilde – Different Interpretations? In Henning Salling Olsen & Jens Højgaard Jensen (eds): *Project Studies – A Late Modern University Reform?* Copenhagen: Roskilde University Press.

Nissen, Thomas (1970): *Indlæring og pædagogik.* [Learning and pedagogy]. Copenhagen: Munksgaard.

Nunes, Terezinha – Schliemann, Analucia Dias – Carraher, David William: *Street Mathematics and School Mathematics.* New York: Cambridge University Press.

OECD (1996): *Lifelong Learning for All.* Paris: OECD.

Piaget, Jean (1952 [1936]): *The Origins of Intelligence in Children.* New York: International Universities Press.

Polanyi, Michael (1966): *The Tacit Dimension.* New York: Doubleday.

Popitz, Heinrich – Bahrdt, Hans Paul – Jüres, Ernst August – Kesting, Hanno (1957): *Das Gesellschaftsbild des Arbeiters.* [Ther worker's picture of society]. Tübingen: JCB Mohr.

Rasmussen, Anders Fogh: (1993): *Fra socialstat til minimalstat – En liberal strategi.* [From a social state to a minimal state – a liberal strategy]. Copenhagen: Samleren.

Reich, Robert B. (1992): *The Work of Nations: Preparing Ourselves for 21st Century Capitalism.* New York: Vintage.

Rogers, Alan (1996): *Teaching Adults.* Milton Keynes: Open University Press.

Rogers, Alan – Illeris, Knud (2003): How Do Adults Learn? A Dialogue. Leicester, UK: NIACE: *Adults Learning,* 15 (3), 24-27.

Rogers, Carl R. (1969): *Freedom to Learn.* Columbus, Ohio: Charles E. Merrill.

Rubenson, Kjell (2003): Adult Education and Cohesion. *Lifelong Learning in Europe,* 8 (1), 23-31.

Rubenson, Kjell (2004): Lifelong Learning: A Critical Assessment of the Political Project. In Henning Salling Olesen (ed): *Shaping an emerging reality.* Copenhagen: Roskilde University Press.

Scavenius, Camilla – Wahlgren, Bjarne (1995): *VUC-profil – Voksenuddannelsescentrenes profil.* [Adult education centre profile]. Copenhagen: Danish Ministry of Education.

Schultz, Majken (2000): Læring og kompetence i videnssamfundet. [Learning and competence in the knowledge society]. In Peter Andersen & Peter Frederiksen (red): *Innovation – Kompetence – Læring.* [Innovation – Competence – Learning]. Frederikshavn: Dafolo.

Schäfer, Ulrich (1988): *International Bibliography of the Project Method in Education 1895-1982,* Part 1. Berlin: Verlag von Wissenschaft und Bildung.

Schön, Donald A. (1983): *The Reflective Practitioner: How Professionals Think in Action.* New York: Basic Books.

Schön, Donald A. (1987): *Educating the Reflective Practitioner.* San Francisco: Jossey-Bass.

Schön, Donald A. (ed) (1991): *The Reflective Turn.* New York: Teachers College, Columbia University.

Senge, Peter M. (1990): *The Fifth Discipline:* The Art and Practice of the Learning Organization. New York: Doubleday.

Shayer, Michael – Adey, Philip (1981): *Towards a Science of Science Teaching*. London: Heinemann Educational.

Simonsen, Birgitte (2000): New Young People, New Forms of Consciousness, New Educational Methods. In Knud Illeris (ed): *Adult Education in the Perspective of the Learners*. Copenhagen: Roskilde University Press.

Usher, Robin (1998): Adult Education and Lifelong Learning in Postmodernity. In Knud Illeris (ed): *Adult Education in a Transforming Society*. Copenhagen: Roskilde University Press.

Usher, Robin (2000): Impossible Identities, Unstable Boundaries: Managing Experience Differently. In Knud Illeris (ed): *Adult Education in the Perspective of the Learners*. Copenhagen: Roskilde University Press.

Usher, Robin – Bryant, Ian – Johnston, Rennie (1997): *Adult Education and the Postmodern Challenge*. London: Routledge.

Vedfelt, Ole (2002): *Ubevidst intelligens – Du ved mere end du tror.* [Unconscious intelligence – You know more than you believe]. Copenhagen: Gyldendal, 2. edition.

Veen, Ruud van der (2003): *Transformative Learning and the Trivialization of Adult Education.* Paper presented at the Transformative Learning Conference, Teachers College, Columbia University, New York, 23-25 October.

Vygotsky, Lev S. (1978): *Mind in Society: The Development of Higher Psychological Processes.* Cambridge, Mass.: Harvard University Press.

Vygotsky, Lev S. (1986 [1934]): *Thought and Language.* Cambridge, Mass.: MIT Press.

Wackerhausen, Steen (1997): The Scholastic Paradigm and Apprenticeship. *Journal of Nordic Educational Research*, 3, 195-203.

Wahlgren, Bjarne (1999): Læringsmiljø [Learning environment]. In Carsten Nejst Jensen (ed): *Om voksenundervisning – grundlag for pædagogiske og didaktiske refleksioner.* [Adult education – fundamentals of educational and pedagogical reflections]. Copenhagen: Billesø & Baltzer.

Wenger, Etienne (1998): *Communities of Practice:* Learning, Meaning, and Identity. Cambridge, Mass.: Cambridge University Press.

Wildemeersch, Danny (1991): Learning from Regularity, Irregularity and Responsibility. *International Journal of Lifelong Education*, 2, 151-158.

Wildemeersch, Danny (1998): Social Learning as Social Change – Social Change as Social Learning. In Knud Illeris (ed): *Adult Education in a Transforming Society*. Copenhagen: Roskilde University Press.

Wildemeersch, Danny (2000): Lifelong Learning and the Significance of the Interpretive Professional. In Knud Illeris (ed): *Adult Education in the Perspective of the Learners*. Copenhagen: Roskilde University Press.

World Bank (2003): *Lifelong Learning in the Global Economy: Challenges for Developing Countries*. Washington D.C.: The World Bank.

Ziehe, Thomas (1984): 'Ich bin heute wohl wieder unmotiviert...' – Zum heutigen Selbstbild von Schülern und Lehrern. ['I am probably again today not motivated...' – about the self image of pupils and teachers]. In F. Bohnsack (ed): *Sinnlosigkeit und Sinnperspective. Die Bedeutung gewandelter Lebens- und Sinnstrukturen für die Schulkrise*. [Mindlessness and mind perspectives: The significance of changed life and mind structures for the school crisis). Frankfurt a.M.: Diesterweg.

Ziehe, Thomas (1987): Die gefährliche Gewöhnung an Langweile. [The danger of being used to being bored]. *Päd.extra*, 6.

Ziehe, Thomas (1997 [1996]): Om prisen på selv-relationel viden – Afmystificeringseffekter for pædagogik, skole og identitetsdannelse. [On the price of self related knowledge – demystification effects in pedagogy, school and identity formation]. In Jens Christian Jacobsen (ed): *Refleksive læreprocesser* [Reflexive learning processes]. Copenhagen: Politisk revy.

Ziehe, Thomas – Stubenrauch, Herbert (1982): *Plädoyer für ungewöhnliches Lernen*. [Pleading for unusual learning]. Reinbek: Rowohlt.

Index